On the Trail of Sherlock Holmes

DEDICATION

To every child who has picked up a magnifying glass and made deductions by inspecting a broken twig, footprint in the mud or scruffy old hat.

On the Trail of Sherlock Holmes

Stephen Browning

PEN & SWORD HISTORY

First published in Great Britain in 2022 by
Pen & Sword History
An imprint of
Pen & Sword Books Ltd
Yorkshire – Philadelphia

Copyright © Stephen Browning 2022

ISBN 978 1 52677 901 4

The right of Stephen Browning to be identified as Author of this work has been asserted by him in accordance with the Copyright, Designs and Patents Act 1988.

A CIP catalogue record for this book is
available from the British Library.

All rights reserved. No part of this book may be reproduced or transmitted in any form or by any means, electronic or mechanical including photocopying, recording or by any information storage and retrieval system, without permission from the Publisher in writing.

Typeset by Mac Style
Printed and bound by CPI Group (UK) Ltd, Croydon CR0 4YY

MIX
Paper from
responsible sources
FSC® C013604

Pen & Sword Books Limited incorporates the imprints of Atlas, Archaeology, Aviation, Discovery, Family History, Fiction, History, Maritime, Military, Military Classics, Politics, Select, Transport, True Crime, Air World, Frontline Publishing, Leo Cooper, Remember When, Seaforth Publishing, The Praetorian Press, Wharncliffe Local History, Wharncliffe Transport, Wharncliffe True Crime and White Owl.

For a complete list of Pen & Sword titles please contact

PEN & SWORD BOOKS LIMITED
47 Church Street, Barnsley, South Yorkshire, S70 2AS, England
E-mail: enquiries@pen-and-sword.co.uk
Website: www.pen-and-sword.co.uk

Or

PEN AND SWORD BOOKS
1950 Lawrence Rd, Havertown, PA 19083, USA
E-mail: Uspen-and-sword@casematepublishers.com
Website: www.penandswordbooks.com

Contents

Acknowledgements		vii
Prologue		viii
Part I:	Sir Arthur Conan Doyle and the Creation of His 'most notorious character', Sherlock Holmes	1
Part II:	The Walks	15
Walk 1	London: Where it all began – a walk in Baker Street and immediate area	15
Walk 2	London: A walk along Northumberland Avenue, up the Strand, Fleet Street and on to St Paul's Cathedral	33
Walk 3	London: Walking along Oxford Street, Regent Street, around Piccadilly Circus and into Haymarket	45
Walk 4	London: Around Tottenham Court Road and into Holborn and Covent Garden	55
Walk 5	London: At the centre of Government – a walk in Westminster and Victoria	63
Walk 6	London: Trafalgar Square, Pall Mall and Mayfair	78
Walk 7	London: A walk around the City and East End	85
Walk 8	Walks and Trips elsewhere… in London; in the UK as a Whole	94

Appendix I: A Timeline of the Stories	110
Appendix II: Some Notable Actors who have Played Holmes over the Years	112
Appendix III: An Alphabetical Sherlock Holmes Miscellany	123
Notes	128
Bibliography	134
Index	137

Acknowledgements

Primary acknowledgement must go to the creator of Sherlock Holmes who inspired the author at the age of about 12, and countless others of every age all over the world, to gain a love of reading and puzzles. As regards this study, thanks to the British Library for courteous and professional assistance and to all the Sherlock Holmes buffs who gave their opinions. I am grateful to the National Archives in Kew, London. Special thanks to Daniel Tink, for permission to use some of his wonderful photographs www.danieltink.co.uk: all other photographs are by the author. Thank you to Laura Hirst at Pen and Sword for handling production. My thanks also to Karyn Burnham for editing and making some excellent suggestions.

Prologue
by Dr John H. Watson

Holmes and I had sat in companionable silence for some time after we finished our excellent meal at Simpson's in the Strand. The Beef Wellington, named in honour of our greatest ever military man, was sublime. When he did not have a case and decided to eat at all, Holmes liked to partake of the very finest cuisine. It was the early spring of 1914, just after seven in the evening and we could see the bustling hoards scurrying along the street below. Some were going home after a very long day, and others just coming out for a night's entertainment.

'Do you think,' Holmes said suddenly, 'that people in a hundred years will remember us?'

'Probably not,' I replied. 'There will be all sorts of wonders, then. Like flying machines and probably devices to instantly communicate, and ships that sail underwater. People will have holiday homes on the moon. Your excellent treatises on cigar ash and bee-keeping will be small change in such a world.'

He had aged of late. I knew he was desperately concerned about the state of the Empire given the current grave situation and only that morning had advised the Prime Minister at Downing Street. He still had those incredible bright eyes each side of his hook-like nose, but his hair was tinged with silver now. My words had annoyed him – that was nothing new – but I cared so much for this man that I indulged in some sentimentality; a trait, among many others, for which I had been often soundly, and unjustly in my opinion, reprimanded. I was, after all, as he had often reminded me during the past twenty-odd years, just an ordinary man who often saw but rarely observed. So, I felt justified in trying in my crude way to add some balm to the situation.

'Maybe, Holmes, maybe, people will pass this place and say: 'Holmes and Watson used to eat there.' Perhaps, even, some folk in a hundred years will walk the streets of London to get a sense of your great gifts and want to *feel* the atmosphere as you solved mysteries and crimes that had beaten the finest brains of Scotland Yard.'

'Why on earth would they do that, Watson?'

'Because, Holmes, you are … you are … indescribable. You are one of a kind. You are unique in the annals of the history of these islands.'

'Just these islands, Watson?' he came back quick as a flash with a cheeky grin. He was mollified.

During our many adventures together, I had noticed that he was surprisingly susceptible to flattery, and I sensed he was a happier man as we strolled the two miles back to Baker Street. I had an idea of writing a book then, of walks around our illustrious capital which his many admirers could use. I could perhaps also add details of other places in Britain which witnessed his extraordinary talents. Alas, although I have started it, demands upon my time in the present dreadful war have prevented its completion and the manuscript, such as it is, remains, among notes for many other stories such as *The Giant Rat of Sumatra* in the vaults of the bank of Cox and Co, the Strand.

It is an idea for a future writer, maybe.

Dr John H. Watson
Undisclosed British Army base, 19 September 1917

Part I

Sir Arthur Conan Doyle and the Creation of His 'most notorious character', Sherlock Holmes[1]

I have had a life which, for variety and romance, could, I think, hardly be exceeded.

Sir Arthur Conan Doyle
Crowborough, 1924

On 22 May 1859, Arthur Ignatius Conan Doyle was born in Edinburgh, Scotland. The family was reasonably prosperous but Arthur's father, Charles Altamont Doyle, was chronically addicted to alcohol. His mother, Mary Doyle, was fond of books and remembered by her son as a wonderful storyteller.

Arthur's boyhood, he wrote later in his life, was spartan at home and more spartan at the Edinburgh school where a tawse-brandishing schoolmaster of the old type made young lives miserable. From the age of 7 to 9 he suffered under this pock-marked, one-eyed rascal who might have stepped, he wrote, 'from the pages of Dickens'.[2]

He was to later tell his firm friend, Bram Stoker, that he produced and illustrated his first book of adventures at the age of 6 and that at this time he also discovered a talent for telling a story and then sharing innumerable episodes right through a whole term if necessary. He retained this ability throughout his school life.

At the age of 9, Arthur's family enrolled him in a Jesuit boarding school in England – Stonyhurst, where he excelled at cricket. Touching letters to his mother survive; he was to write to constantly up to her death in 1920. Conan Doyle considered the general curriculum 'medieval but sound', producing 'as decent a set of young fellows as any other school would do'. Corporal punishments were the norm and he considers that no other boy endured more of it. He graduated at the age of 17, by which time his father's mental health problems and alcohol addiction were becoming too much to deal with in the family. In 1876, Charles Doyle was dismissed from his job and in 1885 was admitted to Montrose Royal Lunatic Asylum.

Arthur decided on a medical career and began studies at the University of Edinburgh where he met Joseph Bell, on whom Sherlock Holmes was subsequently based. In a letter to Bell dated 4 May 1892, Conan Doyle states that it is to him that he owes Sherlock Holmes (also in the letter he expresses interest in Bell's idea for a story about a bacteriological criminal but is worried that the public may not be able to understand it properly). Later in life he would recall how the doctor could look at a patient and comment on features, based solely on observation and logic, that were pertinent to the individual's medical needs (see Walk 1).

There were some fascinating teachers, Joseph Bell for one. Another proved of especial significance because Conan Doyle later used some of his peculiarities when creating the very popular and cantankerous Professor Challenger. His name was Professor Rutherford who, with his Assyrian beard, loud voice and enormous chest, awed the students. He had the habit of starting a lecture before he reached the classroom. On the whole, though, Conan Doyle found his studies between 1876 and 1881 – when he emerged as a Bachelor of Medicine – to be a weary grind, oblique and not sufficiently practical for the education of an effective medical man.

He published his first story, *The Mystery of Sasassa Valley*, at this time.

In 1880 he accepted an opportunity to join a whaling boat, the *Hope*, for a seven-month trip to the Arctic. He went as a surgeon and remarked that it was just as well that he was not called upon to demonstrate his medical talents to any great extent. He thoroughly enjoyed the splendid air and considered that he set sail as a 'big, straggling youth', but returned a 'powerful, well-grown man'.

After another stint at sea – this time aboard a steamer sailing to Africa – and a terrible time joining forces with a doctor who, according to his later writings, had considerable difficulty with the concept of honesty, Dr Arthur Conan Doyle set up in Portsmouth and, after three years of scrimping and saving, found himself master of a quite reasonable medical practice.

The events of his life at this time will bring a smile of recognition to many young people struggling to make their way in the world – how he slung a pan over a gas jet, became an expert in getting many slices from a pound of bacon which, combined with bread, tea and the occasional saveloy, became his staple diet. He 'swapped' his medical services for whatever he could – now with the grocer, now with an aristocratic old lady who gave him china and 'art treasures' (including on one occasion a fine lava jug) and sometimes actually for money. One of the most remarkable items was given to him by an elderly lady patient as he was about to leave Portsmouth. It was a blue and white dish that had been brought to England by her son, who was a sailor on board the *Invincible* during the bombing of Alexandria, and came from the Khedive's palace kitchen; it was her most treasured possession.

Gradually his income rose – from £154 in the first year to £800 after a few years. He tells a wonderful story of falling foul of the Income Tax authorities. In his first year he completed the form showing he was not liable for tax and this was returned to him with 'Most unsatisfactory', scrawled across it. He wrote 'I entirely agree' and returned it once more. This resulted in an appearance before the assessors, which ended in mutual laughter. He did, however, write an article ridiculing the tax system and the dreadful form-filling on different coloured sheets of paper which was designed to torment, as it appeared to him quite incomprehensible.

On 6 August 1885 he married Louisa Hawkins whom he described in *The Stark Munro Letters* (1894) as 'a sweet and gentle girl'.

At around this time Conan Doyle was selling some stories for small amounts – he estimates about £4 on average – to various publications such as *Temple Bar* and *The Boy's Own Paper*, but never more than a few each year.

March 1886 is significant as this was when he began writing *A Study in Scarlet* which, a little over a year later, introduced the world to Sherlock Holmes and John Watson courtesy of *Beeton's Christmas Annual*. He followed this up with *Micah Clarke* and thereby set the scene for the rest of his life where he struggled to write what he considered worthy, even great, literature but all most of the world seemed to want was Sherlock Holmes. Some of his writing at this time also reflected his interest in the afterlife and spiritualism. This is interesting as often people assume that he 'came' to spiritualism as a result of his heart-breaking losses in the Great War, particularly his adored son, Kingsley, but this was not the case.

Writing the Sherlock Holmes stories

In his autobiography *Memories and Adventures*, Conan Doyle talks of his mental process when writing Holmes stories. The first question people apparently asked him is whether or not he knows the ending of a story before writing it, to which he replied that of course, it is necessary to know where you are going before setting off. Then the task is to disguise the outcome by what we today would call various plot devices and red herrings. Finally, it is vital to arrive at the ending using clear and logical steps, not by some freak accident or previously untold piece of information.

> It always annoyed me how, in the old-fashioned detective story, the detective always seemed to get at his results by some sort of lucky chance or fluke or else it was quite unexplained how he got there.
>
> Sir Arthur Conan Doyle talking about Holmes on camera in a unique interview.[3]

He very quickly became famous in America and in 1889 agreed to write stories for *Lippincott's Monthly Magazine* of Philadelphia, which was also organising a British edition. In this context, as discussed in Walk 5, he met and famously got along with Oscar Wilde. The result of this meeting was *The Sign of Four*. He also carried on with his quest for serious literary recognition as he saw it by writing *The White Company* which, reputedly, he considered magnificent, throwing his pen across the room in triumph when he had written the last words, where it left a black smudge upon the duck-egg wallpaper. The manuscript was accepted by *Cornhill* which gave him great satisfaction as he had always dreamed of being accepted by a literary magazine which he regarded as serious.

Conan Doyle subsequently wrote to Joseph M. Stoddart, the editor of *Lippincott's Magazine*, saying how delighted he was with the book. He says that he had Chaucer and Froissart as his guide to the Middle Ages and had additionally read 115 books as research.

In the midst of both literary fame and success as a now thriving doctor came a daughter, Mary. Conan Doyle decided henceforth to specialise in Ophthalmology and after a trip overseas he moved to London and began a practice with no patients – as described in Walk 1. To while away the time, he began to write short stories featuring Holmes.

He also agreed that Sidney Paget should become his illustrator, a decision that resulted in Sherlock Holmes becoming based not on Doyle's original conception of him, but a much more handsome man as he was drawn to resemble Paget's brother, Walter. This image has, by and large, lasted to the present day, although there are other 'new' versions of Holmes that bear little relation to this one, for instance in the CBS version *Elementary* with Jonny Lee Miller, or the 2019 Japanese series *Sherlock: Untold Stories*, directed by Hiroshi Nishitani and starring Dean Fujioka as Holmes and Takonori Iwata as his, at first very unwilling, accomplice; they live in a block of flats called 'Baker Heights'. He also nowadays regularly changes sex; for example, a co-production between HBO Asia and Hulu Japan was responsible for *Miss Sherlock*, premiering in 2018, where both Holmes and Watson are based in Tokyo and played by women (Yuko Takeuchi and Shihori Kanjiya) and which received overwhelming approval on ratings site *Rotten Tomatoes*. He also exists in other forms, one being a manga adaptation of *Kyoto Teramachi Sanjo no Homuzu*, roughly translated as *Holmes of Tokyo* and based on novels written by Mai Mochizuki, which was produced as an anime series to great acclaim from 2018 on *TV Tokyo*.

'…and Watson, his rather stupid friend.'

Sir Arthur Conan Doyle, 1927

Watson has transformed considerably also and is now seen as an able and skilled accomplice as, for example, in the films with Robert Downey Jr as Holmes and Jude Law as Watson; it is similar in the BBC production of *Sherlock* where Martin Freeman often saves Holmes, played by Benedict Cumberbatch, from his inability to relate to ordinary human beings. To begin with he was undoubtedly a duffer, even Conan Doyle himself remarking (unfairly most readers would probably claim) in *Memories and Adventures*, that in seven volumes he never shows one gleam of humour or makes a single joke. That this was a common view is attested by a feature, author not given, in the satirical magazine *Punch* of 21 October 1903, shortly after Holmes had 'returned from the dead'; it is titled 'Justifiable Homicide' and, while welcoming Holmes back, suggests he might gain 'double merit' if he would also strangle Watson. By and large, this take on Watson survived until recent times.

> 'Watson. I'm afraid you're an incorrigible bungler.'
>
> Holmes (Basil Rathbone) to Watson (Nigel Bruce)
> in *The Adventures of Sherlock Holmes*, 1939

Another take on Watson as an idiot going the rounds in Edwardian times was in the parody Picklock Holes and Potson where we find Potson miserable during the period when Picklock Holes is presumed to be dead at the bottom of the Reichenbach Falls and yearns to once more hear Holes calling him 'a numskull'.[4]

In 1891, following recovery from an intense illness, Conan Doyle decided with a great rush of joy to dedicate all his efforts to writing and to leave the doctoring behind. In 1892 came the 'chief event' of his life, the birth of his son, Kingsley. He also made the decision that henceforth all his literary efforts would be towards his finer work and Holmes was therefore killed off at Reichenbach Falls. He was concerned that not killing Holmes would mean that he would be identified for ever with what he called 'a lower stratum of literary achievement'. He had this in mind when he visited Reichenbach with his wife for a short holiday and decided that the awesome falls would make a perfect tomb for his 'most notorious character', even if it meant that his bank balance also took a terrifying fall.

On killing Holmes off, Conan Doyle said that he believed in giving the public less than they wanted and, besides, many novelists had been ruined by being driven into a groove. He wrote that he did not wish to be ungrateful to Holmes as he had been a good friend in many ways. One thing he considered was that reading great literature should leave the reader a better person for having read it and no one can say that, in the higher sense that he means it, having read a Holmes story. At best they will have passed a pleasant half hour or so. Henceforward, he also wanted to write of characters that represented his own views, which Holmes never did. Conan Doyle admitted, though, that he had no idea people would take Holmes' death so much to heart.

Thus Holmes 'died'. Thousands cancelled their *Strand* subscriptions and folklore has it that some people wore black armbands in the street; even his mother, to whom Conan Doyle remained devoted, was appalled. Conan Doyle said that another lady came up to him in the street and said 'You beast!' and there are many other stories, some of which are fantastic but some probably having at least a grain of truth, of similar instances.

A terrible double blow at this time saw Louisa diagnosed with Tuberculosis and the death of his father. His interest in spiritualism intensified as he threw himself into his work and embarked upon a spectacularly successful speaking tour of the United States. Upon returning home, his first *Brigadier Gerard* story was published in *The Strand Magazine* and was warmly received.

Louisa had originally been given only a few months to live but her husband's care saw them both take a trip to Egypt in 1896 where they hoped the warm climate would do her good. In 1897 he saw and fell in love with Jean Leckie, a woman of great beauty and sporting and musical accomplishments. You can make of the relationship what you will, and many people have, but Conan Doyle was to devotedly care for his wife until she died in his arms on 4 July 1906. There is one of a series of parallels here with the life of Charles Dickens, discussed as this study progresses, who also became very attracted to a young woman – Ellen Ternan – while still married; some people believe that this relationship was much more than friendship.

Meanwhile a very busy and complex life saw the four-act play *Sherlock Holmes* starring William Gillette open to critical panning but huge box office success at the Lyceum Theatre in London. When the star asked Conan Doyle if he could take a few liberties with the character he was told: 'You may marry him, murder him, or do anything you like to him.'[5]

Gillette wrote the play himself, principally utilising *A Scandal in Bohemia*, *The Final Problem* and *A Study in Scarlet*, but lifted complete passages of dialogue from the canon; he and Conan Doyle were credited as being co-authors. It premiered in 1899 at the Garrick Theatre in New York (260 performances), went on a tour of the US and opened, as mentioned above, at the Lyceum in London in 1901 (200 performances). Thereafter Gillette revived it a number of times. Conan Doyle thought Holmes was 'wonderfully acted' and was more than satisfied with the contribution the play made to his finances.

A previously lost silent film of Gillette's Holmes, dated 1916, was rediscovered in 2014.

Despite the phenomenal success of his writing at this time, Conan Doyle wrote that his soul was often troubled, that he had another role in life but was unable to see what this might be.

Sherlock Holmes, Sir Arthur Conan Doyle and Sport

Sir Arthur Conan Doyle was an avid sportsman; Holmes certainly was not, regarding such activity as a waste of precious effort. Holmes was, however, a remarkably strong man able to go for considerable lengths of time without food when on the scent in a case and even taking himself close to death in *The Adventure of the Dying Detective*. At the end of the story, Watson remarks upon Holmes' 'ghastly face' when previously laid up in bed, to which Holmes replies: 'Three days of absolute fast does not improve one's beauty, Watson.' That he was a fit runner is clear from *The Hound of the Baskervilles* and that he had great strength is evidenced in *The Adventure of the Speckled Band* when he straightens up a steel poker which had been twisted out of shape by Dr Grimesby Roylott.

Elsewhere we hear of his other physical prowess, extensive where he bothered to develop it but limited in scope. In *The Sign of Four* we are told that he had gone three rounds with the prize fighter, McMurdo, who says that Holmes could have aimed high had he taken up the sport. His boxing skills are also referred to elsewhere in the canon, for example in *The Adventure of the Solitary Cyclist* and *The Naval Treaty*. Conan Doyle regarded boxing as 'the finest single man sport', (rugby football being 'the best collective one, needing strength, courage, speed and resource'). When he needed to bring him back from the dead, Conan Doyle wrote that Holmes had developed a proficiency in bartitsu, the Japanese system of wrestling, and it was this that had proved critical in his fight with Moriarty at Reichenbach Falls. Although he usually left it to Watson to bring a revolver when needed on cases, we know that he could shoot, too, maybe most memorably by decorating Mrs Hudson's wall with 'V.R.' in bullet holes in *The Musgrave Ritual*.

Conan Doyle makes it clear in his writing that he has no time for hunting with guns as a sport, remarking that a brave man and a coward, a strong man or a weak one, can all do it and that no ultimate good comes from killing a creature solely for human amusement.

His great love was cricket, a game which he said had, on the whole, given him more pleasure during his life than any other branch of sport. He is legendary for taking the wicket of the greatest cricketer of the age – W.G. Grace. This was part of a match in August 1900 and he describes his triumph in a poem, *A Reminiscence of Cricket* (1922). He writes of the moment that 'W.G.' as he was known is caught behind the wicket by the keeper, a player called Storer. Conan Doyle bowls the ball, it clips 'W.G.'s bat and:

> I stood with my two eyes fixed on it,
> Paralysed, helpless, inert;
> There was 'plunk' as the gloves shut upon it,
> And he cuddled it up to his shirt.

Conan Doyle does not mention that at the time Grace was 52 years old and had already made a hundred but Sherlockians would regard that as nit-picking.[6]

'W.G.' had his revenge in a subsequent match, bowling Conan Doyle when he went in to bat with a great big looping ball which pitched short, and skidded through to the wicket keeper who quickly whipped off the bails, leaving the startled author wondering for the rest of his days how on earth such a ball could have been played. On another spectacularly memorable occasion – at Lord's, north London, when both 'W.G.' and Conan Doyle were batting alongside each other – a ball from the England bowler Bradley smacked into a small tin vesta box in Conan Doyle's trouser pocket, setting the matches ablaze. 'W.G.' was greatly amused, saying 'Couldn't get you out – had to set you on fire!'

Conan Doyle also had a great deal to do with Olympic matters – firstly as a star reporter on the 1908 Olympic games and then, in 1912, in response to a personal telegram from Lord Northcliffe to the effect that Great Britain must regain her place in the medals table. This resulted in a fair deal of frustration for Conan Doyle as he laboured to bring opposing rancorous factions together and he remarked that he never received one word of thanks from anyone. His efforts included an impassioned letter to the *Evening Standard*, published 22 July 1912, in which he argued that if any of the Empire's 300,000,000 people of all races and colours could fight for Britain in a war, then surely they could represent them at sports during peacetime. Thereafter he vowed to be wary of any telegrams from Lord Northcliffe.

The Boer War and knighthood

Upon the outbreak of the Boer War Conan Doyle startled his friends and family by announcing that he was to sign up as a volunteer doctor and he set sail for South Africa in February 1900. Having treated thousands of soldiers and watched swathes of them die of typhoid, he produced a 500-page report, *The Great Boer War*, in October 1900, in which he made suggestions as to the remedy for serious organisational shortcomings. In two years, this book went through sixteen editions, each modified and updated by the author. This was to lead to his knighthood in 1902 bestowed by Edward VII, who was also reported to be a big Sherlock Holmes fan.

The war experiences and the wish to do something practical may have had a bearing on his decision upon return to enter politics and contest a seat in central Edinburgh; he lost very narrowly, as he did again in a further contest in 1906. He hated what he had to do in the election process as he later made clear, calling it 'a vile business', but chastening, much, he said, like a mud bath.

In 1901 he published, as usual in *The Strand Magazine*, the first part of one of, if not *the*, most famous of Sherlock Holmes tales, *The Hound of the Baskervilles*. The year before he had spent an extended holiday in Cromer, Norfolk, recovering from enteric fever; Cromer being famed for its invigorating bathing and healthy air ever since Jane Austen declared it the 'best of all bathing places' in *Emma* (1815).[7] Although disputed, many locals still believe Cromer to have been the inspiration for the tale as it is suggested that while here he heard of the local legend regarding the Black Shuk, a giant hound with glowing eyes which had been searching for its master since the 1700s and was prone to roam the clifftops at night feeding on the throats of any locals foolish enough to venture out.

> And a dreadful thing from the cliffs did spring,
> And its wild bark thrilled around.
> His eyes had the glow of the fires below,
> 'Twas the form of the Spectre Hound.
>
> Old Norfolk verse

Conan Doyle's 'serious' work, such as his report into the state of the British army and his incredible fictional creations, especially Holmes and his adventures, to say nothing of his indefatigable energy and interest in everything from psychic matters to rifles, did not always sit easily together in the minds of the public. *Punch's Almanack 1904*, for example, produced a humorous piece about his army report, love of dogs, slouch hats, Mauser pistols and the by-now famous hound. It states that by his invention of a 'phosphorescent hound' he has established the right to be considered alongside Edison as an inventor and has immensely strengthened the capabilities of the British Army as at present just a few men with suitable equipment and 'one well-trained phosphorescent dog' are capable of resisting a whole army corps.

In 1903, to the delight (and relief) of his fans, royal and otherwise, around the world, *The Strand Magazine* began serialisation of the stories contained in *The Return of Sherlock Holmes*. Holmes had returned from the dead. Among many poems and articles celebrating his return was one with the refrain: 'Oh Sherlock, Sherlock, he's in town again', and which contained the memorable lines: 'The world of crime has got the blues, / For Sherlock's out and after clues.'

On 18 September 1907, over a year after the death of Louisa, Conan Doyle married Jean Leckie and they moved to a new home – 'Windlesham' in Sussex.

Following his very happy new marriage, Conan Doyle's literary output dwindled, content as he seemed to share activities with his wife. He did, however, write a few plays, mostly unsuccessful but including the money-maker *The Speckled Band*, discussed in Walk 2. His family grew: Denis was born in 1909, followed by Adrian in 1910 and finally Jean in 1912.

In 1912 he gave the world the incredibly entertaining, if impossible, Professor Challenger in *The Lost World*. There followed four more Challenger novels which were very popular, breaking literary ground with aspects of a new genre which was rare at the time – H.G. Wells was already a famous writer in the 'new' genre – but which later came to be popular and known as science fiction.

Sherlock Holmes fans were pleased to see *The Valley of Fear* appear in 1914 but were far from satisfied as the legendary detective is absent from the novel for much of it. He made up for this with the thrilling collection *His Last Bow* in 1917.

In 1914 Sir Arthur and his wife went on a trip to New York, which they didn't like, and then to Canada, which they loved. Upon the outbreak of war, Conan Doyle again offered his services to the military, although he was 55 years of age. This proposal was refused but he kept very active and sent many suggestions on military matters to the War Office, sometimes much to their annoyance as he came to be seen as a nuisance; this included some suggestions for the development and uses of submarines and airships. In 1916 he was given permission to visit the British, French and Australian soldiers on the front, scenes of death and horror that he would never be able to forget. He was to lose his son, Kingsley, and brother, Innes, due to the war.

In 1916 Conan Doyle came to the defence of Sir Roger Casement, accused of being a traitor and, critically perhaps, given the attitudes of the times, a homosexual. He had always found the man likeable and was instrumental in organising a huge petition on his behalf. You can inspect this today in the National Archives at Kew; it is headed: 'TREASON. Sir Roger Casement. Petition for reprieve from Sir Arthur Conan Doyle and other literary persons.' It was unable, however, to save Casement from the gallows at Pentonville prison on 3 August 1916. Conan Doyle maintained that he had never heard Roger Casement say anything to the detriment of Britain, and that any dubious, treasonable actions of which he was accused must have been the result of mental stress.

After the war, Conan Doyle became increasingly involved in promoting spiritualism and the occult, being widely ridiculed, especially over his belief in the veracity of the 'Cottingham Fairies', a series of pictures supposedly taken by two teenage girls in Cottingham, Yorkshire, and which Conan Doyle pronounced genuine. His wife also took up the spiritual crusades, as they were to think of them, and the whole family, including the three children, went on speaking tours of Australia, America and Africa. In all, he spent over a quarter of a million pounds on these activities and in 1926 was forced to shore up his bank balance by writing three more Professor Challenger novels and in 1927, to the joy of Holmes aficionados, *The Casebook of Sherlock Holmes*. In the autumn of 1929, with his health deteriorating and sometimes in considerable pain, he went on a final psychic tour to Holland, Denmark, Sweden and Norway.

> 'Why should we fear a death which we know for certain is the doorway to unutterable happiness?'

> 'Why should we fear our dear ones' death if we can be so near to them afterwards?'
>
> Sir Arthur Conan Doyle

In the spring of 1930 Sir Arthur was found collapsed in his garden, holding a single white snowdrop. On 7 July 1930 he died, convinced that he was going on the greatest journey of all. His last words were to his wife: 'You are wonderful'.

He was buried, following a simple spiritualist ceremony, upright, in his garden at Crowborough, Sussex beside the hut in which he used to write sometimes. He and Lady Doyle had prepared for this moment; you can read, in the National Archives at Kew, the document, 'Sir Arthur Conan Doyle and Lady Doyle, 'Windlesham', Crowborough. Proposed burial in Private Grounds. Sanction. 1930-40'. This will not have helped when the house was sold in 1955, and he, with Lady Doyle, were re-interred in the churchyard at All Saints, Minstead in the New Forest, Hampshire. Reputedly, senior clergy in the Church of England were not very happy, and he was only allowed to rest on the far boundary of the churchyard. 'Steel True, Blade Straight' is inscribed on his tombstone.

Conan Doyle's beliefs about life and death

> 'The Press only unfortunately usually only notices spiritualism when fraud or folly is in question'
>
> Sir Arthur Conan Doyle, 1927

Conan Doyle, in an interview with *Strand Magazine* in March 1919, said he was convinced that our human body has an exact spiritual counterpart and that we were exactly the same five minutes after death as five minutes before, except that any illness or pain had vanished. We were then in a kind of holding place, just like our old life but raised to a 'higher octave' – more pleasant, homely, brighter and more intellectual. Those who had committed evil would need to go on a different route but this was designed to be restorative, not primarily to punish. Then we would go on.

A seance was held at the Royal Albert Hall six days after Conan Doyle's death, attended by thousands and Lady Conan Doyle. He had apparently said that he would return to speak if he could. There was an empty chair on the stage for him. The clairvoyant announced that he was indeed present, in evening dress. She said that he was saying that someone had visited his grave in Crowborough that morning and Lady Doyle said that this was so. Lady Doyle said that she had no doubt whatsoever that he would come back and speak to her when he was ready. That was about it on this occasion, but subsequently some recordings were made at seances of, it is believed, Conan Doyle speaking. The British Library has material, both written and audio-based, on this and it can be accessed by appointment.

Part II

The Walks

WALK 1

London: Where it all began – a walk in Baker Street and immediate area

At A Glance – the following stories, plays and novels are highlighted in this walk:

The Adventure of the Beryl Coronet. A Study in Scarlet. The Adventure of the Blue Carbuncle. The Sign of Four. The Yellow Face. The Hound of the Baskervilles. The Adventure of the Devil's Foot

Distance: If you wish to visit Marylebone Road, Baker Street and perhaps the Sherlock Holmes Museum, having a quick look in Regent's Park before proceeding to Upper Wimpole and Harley Streets you will only walk three kilometres (1–2 miles) at the most. However, Regent's Park is vast and has its own 10km walk as well as London Zoo, so this trip can be extended in both space and time almost as much as you like. There are wonderful picnic spots in the park.

Time to allow: A complete morning or afternoon for the shorter trip but a complete day – or more – if you also wish to explore the attractions of Regent's Park, including the zoo or maybe take in a play in the open-air theatre in the evening.

Walking conditions: Fairly easy and flat but visitors need to be mindful of heavy traffic in Marylebone Road and Baker Street. There are some unique photo opportunities, especially of Baker Street itself.

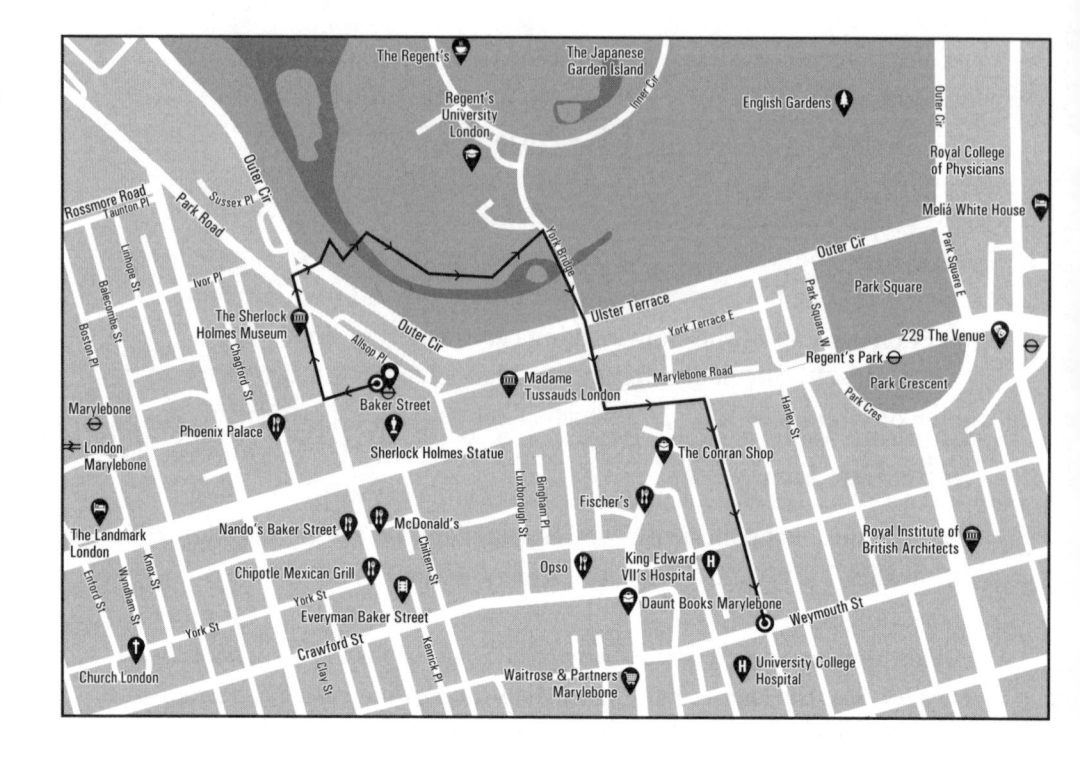

16   On the Trail of Sherlock Holmes

Route
- Baker Street tube station
- Marylebone Road
- Baker Street
- Regent's Park
- Upper Wimpole Street
- Harley Street

Arriving at Baker Street[8]

This walk begins at Baker Street tube station, which is in Zone 1 and served by five lines – Metropolitan, Circle, Hammersmith and City, Bakerloo and Jubilee – and is one of the world's first underground stations, opened in 1863. It is worth a linger on the platforms to see the custom-made tiling celebrating Sherlock Holmes. Numerous buses also stop at Baker Street – a very popular route for tourism purposes is the 139 which travels via Waterloo, Trafalgar Square, Piccadilly Circus and Oxford Circus to Baker Street and beyond.

Baker Street tube station rarely features in the stories as potential clients are more often dramatically observed from the front window of 221B, arriving either on foot or in a cab, allowing for some pertinent deductions to be made prior to a face-to-face meeting with Holmes. An exception, however, is at the beginning of *The Adventure of the Beryl Coronet* when the portly figure of Alexander Holder announces on his arrival 'puffing and blowing' that he has chosen to travel by underground from Threadneedle Street on account of the snow making cab travel very slow.

Immediately outside the station, on Marylebone Road, is a metre-high statue of Holmes by John Doubleday. There has been a campaign, on and off, for a memorial close to Baker Street since G.K. Chesterton had the idea in 1927. This bronze, with deerstalker and pipe which were originally made famous by the illustrations of Sidney Paget in *The Strand Magazine*, was unveiled in 1999; it now has a message for visitors, written by the best-selling author, Anthony Horowitz, which is accessed by scanning a QR code. It was located here as there was no room in Baker Street and it was funded by the Abbey National Building Society whose premises, 215–229 Baker Street, once encompassed 221B.

There are other statues to Holmes: one at Meiringen, Switzerland, also by John Doubleday: at Karuizawa, Japan; Edinburgh, and one of both Holmes and Watson near the British Embassy in Moscow. One of the most successful television series of all time on Russian television has been the superb series *The Adventures of Sherlock Holmes and Dr Watson*, which began in 1979 and starred Vasily Livanov as Holmes and Vitaly Solomin as Watson. Livanov was to receive an honorary MBE (Member of the Most Excellent Order of the British Empire) in 2006 for his portrayal of Holmes and for many fans his interpretation is unsurpassed. This series, with English subtitles, is available to buy on DVD today and clips are available on YouTube.

What did Sherlock Holmes look like?

Conan Doyle was to write late in his life that all the drawings in various publications and impersonations of Holmes 'were very unlike my own original idea of the man'. Conan Doyle saw him as a man with a thin razor-like face and what he called 'a great hawks-bill of a nose' with two small eyes set close together. He said that when he gave the commission to Sidney Paget, the talented artist, who was to tragically suffer a premature death, decided to model Holmes on his handsome younger brother, Walter, and thus was produced a less lean, more handsome but not so powerful conception than his own.

Similarly, there is no mention in the stories of the deerstalker hat, this, too, becoming synonymous with Holmes through Paget's artwork and subsequently by the actors playing Holmes on stage, who loved its dramatic appearance. It is also true that probably the most famous rejoinder in the books – 'Elementary, My Dear Watson' – was never uttered by Holmes: 'Elementary' yes, as well as 'My Dear Watson', but never the two together. Thus, Holmes the fictional creation almost instantaneously entered public consciousness as quite different in important ways from the vision of his creator.

On whom was he based?

There is no doubt about this – Conan Doyle makes it quite clear that he was at least partly based on one of his teachers at the Edinburgh Infirmary, the surgeon Joseph Bell, whose looks, as outlined by Conan Doyle, were not unlike Conan Doyle's original idea. We must be forever grateful that Joseph Bell took Conan Doyle as his outpatient clerk which entailed the marshalling of the patients into a room, taking rough notes on their ailments and then showing them into the great man who appraised them surrounded by admiring students. Conan Doyle was thus to see the most remarkable deductions which Joseph Bell made of the patient's life just by observations (which may have been the origins of Holmes' later common lament to ordinary mortals: 'you see but you do not observe'). Sometimes these would include correct facts about a person's job and where they lived. He told his students to note whether a man removed his hat or not, how he stood, and his general demeanour as these observations could very well lead to preliminary thoughts as to the patient's medical condition. Conan Doyle readily admitted that he used these traits, amplified and refined, in his depiction of Holmes. Bell kept in touch with Conan Doyle for many years, supporting him in his political ambitions and taking an interest in Holmes which included sometimes making suggestions for the stories.

Joseph Bell was modest about his contribution to Sherlock Holmes, declaring that the credit must go to the 'genius' of Conan Doyle. Any patient, he said, was bound to have more confidence in a doctor's ability to cure him in the future if he sees that the doctor knows much of his past, and the trick was much easier than it appeared.

'I thought of a hundred little dodges, as you may say, a hundred little touches by which he could build up his conclusions.'

Sir Arthur Conan Doyle[9]

Conan Doyle was also very aware of two famous literary figures – Edgar Allan Poe's C. Auguste Dupin, who made his first appearance in print in 1841 and Emile Gaboriau's Monsieur Lecoq, a detective employed by the French Sûreté; they are both discussed by Holmes and Watson at the beginning of *A Study in Scarlet*. Another French author, Henry Cauvain published a novel in 1871 about a detective with some characteristics not unlike those of Holmes – depressed sometimes, anti-social and opium-smoking. He is called *Maximilien Heller*. It is not known if Conan Doyle was aware of him but he was fluent in French, so well could have been.

Holmes: for all ages and every era

'My name is Sherlock Holmes. It is my business to know what other people do not know'

The Adventure of the Blue Carbuncle

Holmes has, somewhere in the world, and in differing art forms, been portrayed for every age from junior to elderly. The current *Baker Street Elementary* comic strip, on the back of the newsletters of the *Dallas Sherlock Holmes Society*, features Holmes and Watson as young children in adventures such as 'The Red-Freckled League' and 'A Scandal in Casserole'.[10] *Young Sherlock Holmes*, featuring Holmes as a teenager, is a series of books by Andrew Lane, while the 1985 film *Young Sherlock Holmes*, a cross between the works of Conan Doyle and *Raiders of the Lost Ark*, was written by Chris Columbus and received mixed reviews.

Then, of course, there is the canon itself which takes Holmes from a young university student to elderly bee-keeper on the Sussex Downs; his last imaginary case from here is superbly portrayed by Sir Ian McKellen in the film *Mr Holmes*, directed by Bill Condon and based on a 1985 novel by Mitch Cullins, *A Slight Trick of the Mind*.

He has also time-travelled, especially into the future from Victorian London, saving the world from tyranny in the Second World War, courtesy of the much-loved films starring Basil Rathbone and Nigel Bruce which many fans still regard as *the* pairing. In America CBS' *Elementary*, and in England the BBC's *Sherlock* reinvent Holmes and Watson in the present day, and he solves crimes (at the moment of writing) in Japan in shows such as *Sherlock: Untold Stories* from Fuji Television and *Miss Sherlock* where Holmes and Watson are both women and operate principally in Tokyo. The British/American production of *Sherlock Holmes in the 22nd Century* is a cartoon version of heavily amended tales directed by Paul Quinn – all twenty-six episodes were released on DVD in 2018.

Baker Street

A few yards away from the statue is Baker Street, named after the builder, William Baker, who laid it out in the eighteenth century; it originally housed Madame Tussauds but this subsequently moved to Marylebone Road, a short walk from where you are standing. This is also the home of The Sherlock Holmes Experience, an interactive walk-through exhibit where you are invited to 'find' Sherlock Holmes as he has gone missing. Details at www.madametussauds.com

Just a few yards along Baker Street, on your right, is a block of flats – Chiltern Court – and here are two plaques, one to H.G. Wells (1866–1946) who lived here from 1930–36, and the other to Arnold Bennett (1867–1931) who lived here for the last year of his life.

> 'History is a race between education and catastrophe'
>
> H.G. Wells

While based here H.G. Wells, already world-famous as the author of many books including *War of the Worlds*, *The Time Machine* and *The Island of Dr Moreau*, travelled extensively, visiting President Franklin D. Roosevelt and interviewing Joseph Stalin – the interview reputedly lasted three hours and was enjoyed by its subject – for the *New Statesman*. He predicted a world war before 1940 and was critical of Hitler, which resulted in his books being banned in public libraries in Germany from 1933. He said: 'The man who raises a fist has run out of ideas.' He was on the list of people subject to immediate arrest in the event of a successful Nazi invasion of Britain.

Conan Doyle knew and very much liked another Roosevelt – Theodore (26th American President 1901–9). For Conan Doyle he occupied a prominent place among all the great figures of the time, of whom he knew a good few. He is described by Conan Doyle as not a big or powerful man, but one who had 'a tremendous dynamic force and iron will'. He had 'the simplicity of real greatness, speaking his mind with great frankness and in the clearest possible English', and 'a quick blunt wit'. On one occasion, Conan Doyle recounts, when Roosevelt was awoken to address some people who had assembled at a wayside railway station, his assistant remarked that they had travelled sixty miles to see him. 'They would have come a hundred to see a cat with two heads,' Roosevelt replied.

Sir Arthur Conan Doyle knew Wells for many years, preceding his knighthood by a long way, and remarked that he must have often entered the draper's shop in which Wells was employed at Southsea. He regarded Wells as 'one of the great fruits which popular education has given us', but observes that 'his democratic frankness and complete absence of class are occasionally embarrassing'.

Arnold Bennett was a prolific writer and journalist, his most convincing works highlighting the lives of working people in the Staffordshire Potteries. He famously remarked that he was not just concerned with art for art's sake, but in 'pocketing two guineas a piece' for magazine stories which he was better able than many to compose. Of his novels, *Riceyman Steps*, published in 1923, is possibly the most renowned. His work as a whole was controversial during his lifetime with critical acclaim often eluding him until half a century after his death. He died of typhoid in the Baker Street flat on 27 March 1931 having returned from Paris where he is reputed to have drunk a glass of infected tap water.

What of the literary scene during which Sherlock Holmes was created? Conan Doyle was aware that the London press was not impressed with the crop of authors that followed Dickens and Thackeray. Conan Doyle, however, considered the current batch when he began writing his Holmes stories to be as talented and varied as at any other time in Britain's history. He admired Oscar Wilde, Rudyard Kipling – he wrote later in life how in the Southsea days, despite being an impecunious young doctor he nevertheless bought and loved Kipling's first book, *Plain Tales from the*

Hills – Hall Caine, Anthony Hope, James Stephen Phillips, Bernard Shaw, Grant Allen, Barrie, H.A. Jones, Pinero, Marie Corelli, Stanley Wayman, Winston Churchill and H.G. Wells. Ironically, the preservation of his home 'Undershaw' was later in doubt (although saved from being demolished to make way for flats in the end – see Walks and Trips 8) as the authorities expressed the view that Conan Doyle was not quite in the same literary league as Dickens.

He was subsequently a great fan of Bram Stoker's *Dracula*, writing to the author on 20 August 1897 congratulating him on sustaining such a high level of excitement over such a long period – a feat for which Conan Doyle himself would be celebrated following the publication of *The Hound of the Baskervilles*.

People from all over the world come to see the Sherlock Holmes Museum which is on your left about three quarters of the way along – often it is easily visible at the head of an uncharacteristically chatty and happy queue snaking back down the street. There is usually a 'policeman' outside who will lend you his helmet for a photo before ushering you in. The house is a recreation of the home that Holmes occupied from 1881–1904 and is open every day except Christmas Day from 9.30am to 6pm. Try to arrive as soon after opening time as possible for a quicker entry. Tickets are not available from the internet but must be bought at the door; at the time of writing they cost £15 per adult and £10 for a child under 16. (www.sherlock-holmes.co.uk). There are some interesting videos on YouTube, worth checking out before you come, from fans who have visited the house.

221B Baker Street

We are introduced to the rooms at 221B Baker Street in *A Study in Scarlet*. Watson, returned from the 2nd Afghan war, has gravitated to London, 'that great cesspool into which all the loungers and idlers of the Empire are irresistibly drained'. He stays for a while at a private hotel in the Strand and finds that his income of eleven shillings and sixpence a day to be woefully inadequate. He meets Holmes – as detailed in Walk 7 – and agrees to share rooms. They comprised a couple of comfortable bedrooms and a large airy sitting room 'cheerfully furnished' with two broad windows overlooking the street. They were so desirable that Watson moved his things in the evening of the same day.

'I've written a good deal more about him than I intended to do, but my hands have been forced by kind friends'

Sir Arthur Conan Doyle, talking of Holmes

A perfect Sherlock Holmes adventure?

For many fans, the perfect Sherlock Holmes story should either start or end at 221B (or preferably both). Perhaps to begin with the wind is howling outside, shaking the windows; maybe the snow is falling or there is a pea-souper so bad that Watson, gazing from the inside of the front room warmed by a roaring fire, can hardly see the houses opposite. The doorbell will clang, there will be a clatter of footsteps and a perplexed client will almost fall into the room to be revived by a glass of medicinal brandy and water. Or at the end of a case a grateful Lestrade, or maybe Hopkins, will call and over drinks, or while Mrs Hudson prepares a fine English roast dinner which includes roast potatoes and all the trimmings, Holmes will hold court explaining the finer points of his latest triumph. In 1942 Vincent Starrett wrote a famous poem, incorporating these features, entitled '221B'. It ends with the lines:

> Here, though the world explode, these two survive,
> And it is always eighteen ninety-five.

Of the fifty-six stories and four novels, over two thirds start at 221B, and almost half end there.[11] Some of the most memorable both begin and end there and a favourite in this category for many, especially at Christmas time, is *The Adventure of the Blue Carbuncle*, published in *The Strand Magazine* in January 1892. It has all of the classic features of a thrilling Holmes adventure. It begins with Watson calling upon Holmes two days after Christmas to wish him the compliments of the season. There is a sharp frost outside and a crackling fire within and Homes is 'lounging upon the sofa in a purple dressing gown'. A master class in deduction follows, featuring a battered billycock hat, before a tale unfolds about the robbery of a fabulous gem, the Countess of Morcar's Blue Carbuncle. A man has been – unjustly – accused and Holmes must find the real culprit. This entails a rush to track a particular goose through the centre of London, an area which Conan Doyle knew in detail, featured in this study in Walks 2, 3 and 4 – Wimpole Street, Harley Street, Wigmore Street, Oxford Street, Covent Garden and Holborn – and brilliant deductions from Holmes along with the outwitting of an angry and suspicious market trader. The villain is tricked into coming to Baker Street where he is exposed. In this particular tale, Holmes acts as both judge and jury letting the man go saying: 'I suppose that I am committing a felony, but it is just possible that I am saving a soul', as the man is terrified and unlikely to commit any further crimes. The reader is left to imagine the wonderful meal and festive good cheer that seals this latest triumph as Watson is asked to 'have the goodness to touch the bell, Doctor', so as to begin another investigation 'in which a bird will also be the chief feature'.[12]

221B is also where we are noisily introduced to The Baker Street Irregulars, a group of street-wise young urchins led by Wiggins, originally introduced in *A Study in Scarlet* in 1887. They also appear elsewhere in the stories, notably in *The Sign of Four* where they have a chapter to themselves. Here they invade 221B and clatter up the stairs in their bare, dirty feet causing Mrs Hudson to raise her voice 'in a wail of expostulation and dismay'. Henceforth, Holmes decides that they can report to Wiggins and then he only will in turn report to Holmes. In *The Sign of Four* they are dispatched to find the steam launch *Aurora* as Holmes explains that they are able to mingle almost unobserved among sections of the population where others would stand out. They have gone on to have several of their own spin-off television series and the name 'The Baker Street Irregulars' is used by the prestigious literary society founded in the United States by Christopher Morley in 1934.[13]

Life for the young poor in Victorian and Edwardian England, often portrayed in novels as lovable ragamuffins like the Artful Dodger in Charles Dickens' *Oliver Twist*, was generally brutal and short. If a child managed to survive infancy, he or she may well not reach 20. Cholera, TB and Smallpox were rife. Many believed that disease was carried in putrid air, which largely accounts for the panic caused by the Great Stink of 1858, discussed in Walk 5. The law that made smallpox vaccination compulsory was often flouted and public opposition led to a new Act in 1907, after which parents were no longer forced to have their children vaccinated. There was a great fear as to the side effects of being vaccinated and Conan Doyle wrote to the press on several occasions opposing such fears, pointing out on one occasion when he wrote to the local newspaper in Portsmouth and Southsea, where he was a young doctor, that some parents erroneously attributed any illness whatsoever in their children to the prick of a pin.

Holmes as a living being

Conan Doyle was aware that Holmes was seen by many as a living being. He found this a little silly and said that it initially struck home when a group of schoolboys from France visited London and were asked what they would like to see first; they replied that they wished to see Sherlock Holmes' lodgings in Baker Street. He also found it strange, when on retiring Holmes to the Sussex Downs to keep bees, he received a letter from a lady applying to become Holmes' housekeeper as she was an expert in 'segregating the Queen' ('Whatever that is' continued Conan Doyle).

Letters addressed to Sherlock Holmes have arrived at 221B since his creation. They come from people all over the globe, seeking help and guidance. It is said that a member of staff of the Abbey National Building Society – the HQ of which for some years incorporated the number 221B – was employed to answer the letters and would sometimes say that Sherlock Holmes had now retired to Sussex to keep bees, or perhaps reply using quotes from the stories. Many were from schoolchildren, some tongue-in-cheek but others seemingly not so; Holmes has been asked his opinion on everything from Watergate to Coronavirus. Any that arrive now are directed to the Sherlock Holmes Museum.

Conan Doyle remarked that these letters came to Holmes from the very beginning. They would sometimes be addressed to him with the request that he forward them on to Sherlock Holmes. A great many came from Russia. Others he remembered well included those from a young lady correspondent who began all her letters 'Good Lord'. On one occasion, a touching letter from Warsaw pleaded for some Sherlock Holmes books as they were the chief pleasure of a bedridden invalid. Touched by this, Conan Doyle packed up a set for posting but ran into a fellow author to whom he told the story. The fellow author, with a cynical smile, produced an identical letter from his pocket, leaving Conan Doyle aghast and wondering at the extent of the self-proclaimed lady invalid's library if she had also committed this fraud on other writers. Apparently Watson, too, had letters which were requests for Holmes' autograph. An agency, specialising in press cuttings of the rich and famous, also wrote to Watson asking if Holmes might find it worthwhile to subscribe.

From a study at the National Archives in Kew, it is apparent that letters, primarily from Russia, Romania and Czechoslovakia were also sent to Scotland Yard from the very beginning of Holmes' fame, usually asking if Sherlock Holmes existed and what might be his address. Copies of replies from the Yard can still be seen stating that Sherlock Holmes exists in fiction only and thus regretfully his address cannot be supplied.

An interesting incident occurred following Conan Doyle's knighthood when he was surprised to receive a bill from a tradesman addressed to 'Sir Sherlock Holmes'. He was irate at first, but upon tackling the tradesman could not help bursting out with laughter as the poor man really thought that he was entitled to take that name on the awarding of the honour.

That Holmes is a real person, Watson his biographer and Conan Doyle merely a literary agent who ensured publication is called the Great Game, the Sherlockian Game, the Holmesian Game or simply the Game, and helps to some extent to explain why fact and fiction regarding Sherlock Holmes intermingle. The first essays on this subject saw the light of day in 1902. Dorothy L. Sayers, creator of Lord Peter Wimsey, writes that the Game 'must be played as solemnly as a county cricket match at Lord's; the slightest touch of extravagance or burlesque ruins the atmosphere.'[14]

The Clarence Gate entrance to Regent's Park is literally a few minutes by foot from 221B. We know that Watson in particular liked his constitutionals here but one they both enjoyed together was for two hours, in silence mainly, 'as befits two men who know each other intimately', at the beginning of *The Yellow Face*. The park is one of the Royal Parks, named after the Prince Regent (1762–1830). A wonderful picnic spot, it has walkways and lakes and is home to over 100 species of wild bird – feeding them is now discouraged as this inadvertently does more harm than good. For the energetic there is a 10km sign-posted walk which you can pick up by crossing Clarence Bridge ahead of you and begins slightly to the left as you enter. The park also houses London Zoo and an open-air theatre featuring a range of plays from May to September; a favourite for many visitors is watching a Shakespeare play in the open air on a summer's evening.

The first stories featuring … Sherringford Holmes

If you wish to see the area of London where Conan Doyle first took up a medical practice, leave Regent's Park by the York Bridge exit – a little way along from where you entered (there are clear direction boards) – and make your way south past the Royal Academy of Music Museum and into Devonshire Place, which continues as Upper Wimpole Street and is parallel to the word-famous Harley Street. Conan Doyle wrote in his 1924 autobiography Memories and Adventures that his ophthalmic practice began at number 2 Devonshire Place. He was soon, he writes, to discover that they were both, in fact, waiting-rooms. It was here that he began to while away the hours by writing the adventures of a new kind of consulting detective whom he christened Sherlock Holmes. At first he favoured the name 'Sherringford' but changed it, possibly because he knew a cricketer called Shacklock (later in 1900, while mulling over the plot for *The Hound of the Baskervilles* and playing golf at Sheringham Royal Golf Club in Norfolk, it is likely he came across another club member who was called Moriarty). When writing these initial stories, like Holmes in the early days, Conan Doyle was living close to the British Museum. Every morning he would walk from Montague Place to the consulting rooms and sit there until three or four with absolutely no interruption by way of the receptionist's bell.

The naming of Holmes and Watson happened like this; after he decided to change 'Sherringford' to 'Sherlock', he needed an educated but rather mundane name for his sidekick and Watson had about the right associations. Subsequently he was quite rude about Watson, calling him dull and humourless, but this rather bland template has enabled a fabulous array of interpretations, many – especially the more recent ones as outlined in various parts of this study – almost as quirky and sharp as Holmes himself. Once Conan Doyle had his two main characters named and had a broad idea of their function, he tells us that he was ready to begin *A Study in Scarlet*.

Was Holmes like Conan Doyle?

In the 1920s Conan Doyle was to answer the question that he was asked many times – how similar in personality was Holmes to himself? He said that while he cannot claim to be Holmes' equal in problem solving, there must, of necessity, be some characteristics which transfer from author to fictional character and it is this which lends credibility to the creation. He jokes that this may be a dangerous admission for someone who had created so many criminals and quotes his own poem *The Inner Room*:

> There are others who are sitting,
> Grim as doom,
> In the dim ill-boding shadow
> Of my room.
> Darkling figures, stern or quaint,
> Now a savage, now a saint,
> Showing fitfully and faint
> Through the gloom.[15]

It is interesting that Joseph Bell, who Conan Doyle himself regarded as the main influence on the character of Holmes, thought he could detect Holmes in Conan Doyle himself.

Conan Doyle as Holmes: 1. The incredible Edalji case

Was Conan Doyle able to act as Holmes in real life? There are two celebrated cases where he tried to and the Edalji case is the first in which he did, indeed, prove the innocence of a man accused of shocking cruelty to animals.

George Edalji was brought up in Great Wyrley, north of Birmingham and, despite struggling with racial prejudice – his father was a Parsee Indian who had converted to Christianity and become a vicar – was a conscientious student at Walsall Grammar School and became a successful solicitor. In 1901 he published a well-regarded book (still available on Amazon and elsewhere): *Railway Law for 'the man in the train': chiefly intended as a guide for the travelling public on all points like to arise in connection with the railways.*

He was by all accounts an excellent solicitor and gained many local people and businesses as clients. He was also a lonesome individual who liked to take long solitary walks, upon one of which he was badly beaten up by a gang of roughs; he had no connection to them and racial prejudice was probably involved. In 1903 he was convicted of a terrible crime. Sheep, cows and at least one pony were being mutilated and, slashed with a razor across their stomachs, left to bleed to death. The crimes became known as 'The Great Wyrley Outrages'. George Edalji was convicted and sentenced to seven years' prison with hard labour. However, many people were not convinced of his guilt, a petition was started and, after three years, without any explanation or apology, he was released.

While happy to be released, Edalji was unable to continue in his profession as a solicitor and thought he was entitled to some compensation. He published his story in the press. It was now 1906 and Conan Doyle, reading about the events of the prosecution, saw what seemed to him an innocent man condemned. He felt compelled to help. All appeared clear; the razors found in the Edalji household were merely rusty and could not be linked to those used to mutilate the animals; the soil found on Edalji's clothes and boots was of a different type to that where the last mutilations occurred; a key expert witness on handwriting – taunting letters had been sent after the crimes – was found to have made a serious error of judgement in a former trial which resulted in an innocent man going down; and, damningly one would have thought, the killings and letters continued after Edalji had been accused.

All straightforward so far, but what completely convinced Conan Doyle of Edalji's innocence was a classic Holmesian observation. He had arranged to meet the man at a hotel in 1907 but was late. When he arrived, he noticed when approaching that Edalji had picked up a newspaper to pass the time and was reading it in an unusual way – he held it very close to his eyes and slightly sideways, a clear sign that he suffered from myopia and astigmatism. It was patently absurd to think that such a man could roam the fields at night seeking animals to slaughter, all the while, at least in the later stages of the crimes, avoiding the policemen – at least six sometimes – who had been sent to keep an eye on Edalji at his home and prevent him from venturing out.

Conan Doyle wrote of his observations and conclusions in detail and sent them to the *Daily Telegraph*, making it plain that they were copyright-free so that anyone could use the material. He said that the case amounted to a national scandal.[16] The result was that, although no procedure existed at the time for a retrial, a committee was set up to consider the case afresh. Edalji was cleared of the killings but still found guilty of writing the letters. The Law Society, more wisely, looked at the newly presented facts and permitted Edalji to resume his practice as a solicitor.

This case was one of the factors that resulted in the Court of Criminal Appeal being established in 1907.

Conan Doyle continued his investigations into who the genuine guilty party might be and made the case that it was a man, now a butcher, who had been at school with Edalji; no one, however, was ever charged.[17]

Conan Doyle as Holmes: 2 The Oscar Slater case

Conan Doyle remarked that this case came about as he was generally held responsible for the exoneration of George Edalji and could not refuse to assist in such a grave injustice. Despite all, there was a marked sense of bitterness at the end between Oscar Slater and the famous author.

On 21 December 1908, Glasgow witnessed the gruesome murder of 83-year-old Miss Marion Gilchrist. Her maid had stepped out for a newspaper and when she returned found her employer bludgeoned to death; her papers had been rifled through and a diamond brooch stolen. Five days later the police announced that they were looking for a man who lived nearby: Oscar Slater. He had recently pawned a diamond brooch and, damningly, had left for America under a false name. He was subsequently located in America and agreed to return and face trial, convinced that a misunderstanding had occurred and would quickly be cleared up.

Despite the fact that the diamond brooch he had pawned did not match the one stolen and that he had an alibi for the time of the murder, his previous many criminal activities counted against him[18] and in 1909 he was found guilty and sentenced to be hanged. Two weeks prior to his execution and after a public petition, his sentence was changed to life imprisonment with hard labour.

Slater's lawyers contacted Conan Doyle who at once saw that the evidence did not stack up. With his legendary energy, Conan Doyle found the time to compile a book *The Case of Oscar Slater* which he published in 1912. It refuted the evidence in true Sherlock Holmes style, point by point. One interesting observation was that Slater travelled to America under an assumed name as he was travelling with his mistress and was fearful of his wife, not the police; the world-renowned author was also able to point out as a medical man that the weapon that was found in Slater's possession and which the prosecution alleged caused Miss Gilchrist's death, a light hammer, was far too small to have inflicted the extensive bloody injuries sustained and these were probably caused by something much larger, like a chair leg. It also seemed that the lady opened the door to her murderer and allowed him/her to enter (suspicion later fell on her nephew who was never convicted). Yet another witness testified that Slater was elsewhere at the time of the murder. Conan Doyle was outraged that the authorities refused to reopen the case. Years went by and Conan Doyle continued to press for a retrial when he had an opportunity.

In 1925 a message, smuggled out of prison by Slater courtesy of a released inmate, who hid the message under his tongue, begged Conan Doyle not to forget him and this resulted in a new flurry of letters and pleadings. In 1927 a new book, *The Truth About Oscar Slater* by journalist William Park, changed everything. On 8 November 1927 Slater was released and following a reopening of the case, for which Conan Doyle contributed £1,000 towards costs, Slater was cleared of all charges and awarded £6,000 in compensation.

Conan Doyle was horrified when Slater refused to repay those, including himself, who had contributed money towards his legal fees. It was not the money itself but the lack of honour involved. It was incomprehensible to him that anyone could act in such a manner and be so ungrateful. He wrote a scathing letter to Slater. Slater died in 1948 at the age of 78.

Further contemporary details are available in a file held in the National Archives at Kew: '*Oscar Slater. Correspondence including with Sir Arthur Conan Doyle on case and on mediums*'.

A question of quality

'Ah, what a dusty answer gets the soul when hot for certainties in this our life!'

George Meredith.

Conan Doyle was fascinated by writers and what separates the good from the great. One who interested him all his life was George Meredith[19] and on 20 November 1888 he gave a talk about him to The Portsmouth

Literary and Scientific Society in Portsmouth Guildhall. One of his fellow speakers, by chance, was a Dr Watson. He considered George Meredith admirable at his best, but so bad at his worst that he feared this would drag down his work in the opinion of posterity. There are three things, Conan Doyle believed, which render a story very good – the first is that it is intelligible, the second that it is interesting and the third that it is clever. Dickens and Thackeray fulfil all three conditions but Meredith, alas, only the third. He also said that precise thought makes for precise writing and muddy thought will never do.

As regards the quality of the Sherlock Holmes stories, there is an oft-quoted story, told to Conan Doyle, of a Cornish boatman remarking that when Sherlock Holmes went over the Reichenbach Falls he may not have died but he must have injured himself in some way as the stories thereafter were not quite as good as before. Conan Doyle's belief, however, was that he kept up the standard and that any unprejudiced person, reading them backwards in their entirety, would agree that the last was as good as the first. It is true, though, that some share the same plot idea, notably *The Red-headed League* (*1891*), *The Stock-broker's Clerk* (1893) *and The Adventure of the Three Garridebs* (1924), all of which involve the removal of a person from his usual haunts to somewhere else so that a crime can be committed.

A Study in Scarlet was the first Holmes story to be written and Conan Doyle was pleased with it, having made it the best he could (unlike previous half-hearted attempts at stories). He was disappointed when it took what he called 'the circular tour' back to his home having been rejected by several publishers. There was one left, however, who specialised in cheap and sensational works – Ward, Locke and Co. – and off to them it went. They accepted it, offering a paltry £25 for the copyright and it finally appeared in *Beeton's Christmas Annual* 1887.[20]

The final location in this walk is Harley Street and, famous then and now for medical matters, it features in one of the tales. It was in the spring of 1897 that Holmes' health was critical and he consulted Dr Moore Agar of Harley Street, 'whose dramatic introduction to Holmes I may someday recount…', adds Watson. Holmes had not the slightest interest in his state of health but was nonetheless persuaded to take a complete break. This led to a trip to the West Country and the 'Cornish horror' as Holmes put it: *The Adventure of the Devil's Foot*.

WALK 2

London: A walk along Northumberland Avenue, up the Strand, Fleet Street and on to St Paul's Cathedral

At A Glance – the following stories, plays and novels are highlighted in this walk:

The Hound of the Baskervilles. The Greek Interpreter. The Adventure of the Noble Bachelor. The Adventure of the Illustrious Client. The Adventure of Wisteria Lodge. The Adventure of the Golden Pince-Nez. A Scandal in Bohemia. The Adventure of the Bruce-Partington Plans. The Final Problem. The Adventure of the Missing Three-Quarter. The Adventure of the Speckled Band. The House of Temperley. Fires of Fate. The Tragedy of Korosko. Brigadier Gerard. The Adventure of the Dying Detective. The Red-headed League. The Sign of Four. The Man with the Twisted Lip

Distance: About 3 kilometres/1.8 miles

Time to allow: At least a complete morning or afternoon; if you plan to have a drink or meal in one of the dozens of cafes, restaurants and pubs en route, get a little lost in some of the alleyways off Fleet Street, and/or take in St Paul's, a complete day is more realistic. It is a wonderful walk and distractions abound; notably, you will pass within yards of the Adelphi, Lyceum and other theatres so the walk can be combined with a matinee or evening performance (try the cut-price ticket kiosk in Leicester Square on the day of the show or up to a week in advance; near Leicester Square underground station).

Walking conditions: Very busy, obviously, with buses, cars and thousands of people everywhere. Northumberland Avenue has a slight upward gradient but from the Strand to St Paul's it is pretty flat, although you have to cross some major junctions, for example at Aldwych. Take a camera!

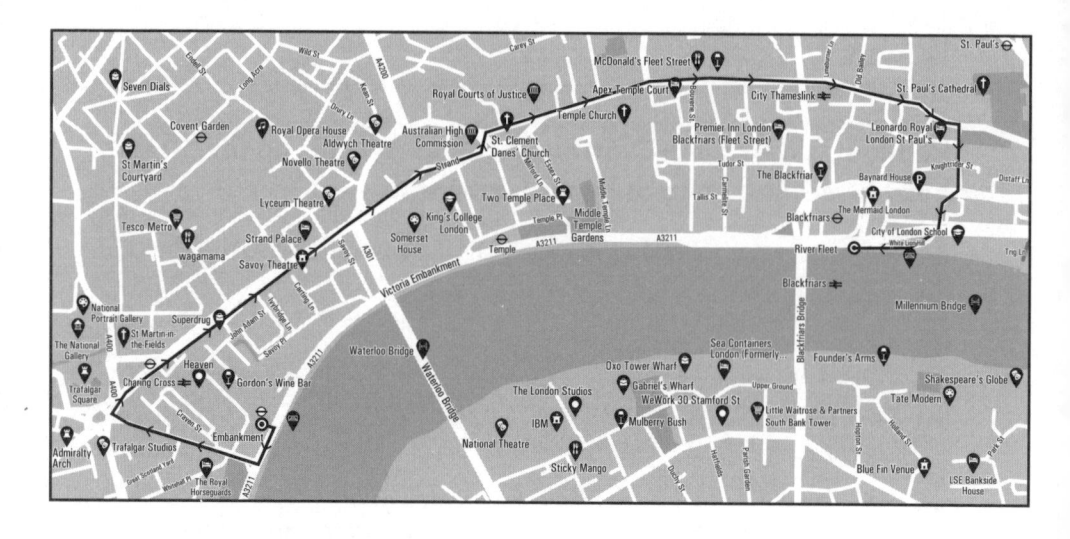

Route

- Embankment tube station
- Northumberland Avenue
- Strand
- Fleet Street
- Ludgate Hill
- St Paul's Cathedral
- St Paul's Wharf

We begin the walk at Embankment tube – District (green), Circle (yellow), Bakerloo (brown) and Northern (black) lines. If you arrive at Charing Cross station, walk the few hundred yards down Villiers Street to the Embankment. Turn right on leaving the station entrance and then turn right again into Northumberland Avenue, a grand leafy thoroughfare leading up to Trafalgar Square. It features in several of the adventures, perhaps most famously in *The Hound of the Baskervilles* when Sir Henry Baskerville, newly arrived at Waterloo station, checks into the Northumberland Hotel, where he mysteriously has his boot stolen from outside his room.

There are several contenders for Sir Henry's Hotel. Northumberland Avenue was designed as a hotel venue from the 1880s on land previously occupied by Northumberland House, home of the Percy family, Dukes of Northumberland. Among the finest hotels were the Grand, the Metropole and the Victoria. Prince Albert, later Edward VII, was a regular visitor to the Metropole; both the Grand and the Victoria had over 500 bedrooms and the latter generated its own electricity through dynamos. In Sherlock Holmes' day, Thomas Edison's UK headquarters was also here, and many famous politicians and actors made speech and song recordings. Subsequently, the government, notably the War Office, took over much of the accommodation. Today it is a mixed area of hotels, corporate entertainment venues and offices. It is a very wide road because for a while planning regulations dictated that new buildings could not exceed in height the width of the thoroughfare.

In *The Greek Interpreter* we learn that Mr Melas was able to obtain clients from among the wealthy Orientals that frequented the Northumberland Avenue hotels. The hotels feature once again in the latter stages of *The Adventure of the Noble Bachelor* where Holmes explains that he was able to trace the man he sought as he knew that he had recently settled his bill at one of the most select hotels in London. As there were not many that charged 'eight shillings for a bed and eightpence for a glass of sherry', he investigated Northumberland Avenue and in the second hotel he tried found that Francis H. Moulton, an American, had left only the day before. It was the vital clue he was looking for and he quickly wraps up the case. On another occasion, Watson was walking alone along Northumberland Avenue between the Grand Hotel and Charing Cross Station in *The Adventure of the Illustrious Client* when he saw the placard on a news stand with the terrible headline, black on yellow background, telling of a physical attack on Sherlock Holmes. Badly shaken, he grabbed a paper without paying for it, then paid, and retreated to the doorway of a chemist's shop to read the dreadful news report in full.

Conan Doyle tells the following story. Once he was staying at the Northumberland Avenue Hotel – probably not one of the above; apart from anything else he was a very practical man and would likely have balked at the expense. One evening he took a walk down by the Embankment and saw a man in a distressed state who appeared to be about to jump in the river. He threw himself towards the man and managed to grab hold of his knees. Leading him across the road he learned that there had been a domestic upset, but the main cause of the would-be jumper's distress was that his business – the man was a baker – was in trouble. Conan Doyle did his best to console the man and gave him some money, 'such immediate help as I could', and having obtained a promise from the man that he would go home and keep in touch, returned to his hotel. He was then troubled by the thought that he had been the victim of a clever swindler and was relieved a few days later to receive a letter from the man, giving name and address.[21]

About halfway up this grand thoroughfare, on the right-hand side, is the Sherlock Holmes Pub. This is undoubtedly the most famous pub associated with Holmes in the UK, but there are others around the world also – including in Budapest, Hungary; Bagarmossen, Sweden; and Pistoia, Italy. The Sherlock Holmes pub serves English pints and traditional food and the tables outside are a great place to sit and watch people going about their business on Northumberland Avenue. Inside is a recreation of Holmes' sitting room and a unique collection – first put together for the Festival of Great Britain 1951 – of Sherlockian artefacts.

Around here somewhere would have been the Turkish Bath establishment visited by Holmes and Watson as *The Adventure of the Illustrious Client* begins. It was on an upper floor but we do not have the exact address. Some Sherlockians claim that the entrance is on Craven Street which leads off the avenue at this point. Craven Street is also the location of the Mexborough Private Hotel where, in *The Hound of the Baskervilles*, Stapleton kept his wife imprisoned in her room while, disguised by wearing a beard, he followed Dr Mortimer to Baker Street and then to the Northumberland Hotel, all the while planning the demise of Sir Henry Baskerville. It is the perfect spot, tucked away and yet right at the centre of his evil web, so to speak. The other claim to fame of this narrow street, of particular interest to American visitors, is that here was the home of Benjamin Franklin for much of the period 1757–75, although exactly where is not universally agreed – possibly one of the houses numbered 27 or 36.

Conan Doyle himself was fond of a Turkish Bath and recounts an amazing incident, worthy of a Holmes story, of a very unusual one at which he just happened to bump into the Prime Minister of Great Britain. It occurred when he was staying with Lord Burnham who had a Turkish bath in the front of his house with a drying room next door. Conan Doyle had finished his bath, arrayed himself in a long towel with another screwed around his head and was in the drying room when the door opened and in walked Arthur Balfour, Prime Minister of England. Not knowing the house, it is possible that Balfour entered the room in error. He looked with amazement at Conan Doyle who raised the towel on his head in greeting. Not a word was said and the Prime Minister left the room.[22]

Another Prime Minister he knew, and played golf with (he was apparently not very good) was Mr Asquith,[23] whom he admired as a sweet-tempered man who said little but lived up to what he did say.

At the top, ahead of you, you will see Nelson standing on top of his column; Trafalgar Square is discussed in detail in Walk 6. Here the walk turns right into the Strand. The traffic – private cars, taxis and buses – and the throngs of people is pure bedlam, so it is essential to cross the roads using the pedestrian crossings. Once into the Strand, the pavements are slightly less crowded and also flat.

The Strand takes its name from the old English word 'strond', meaning the edge of a river; here, from the twelfth to the seventeenth centuries the rich and powerful owned mansions that stretched down to the river, each with a private mooring. Thereafter it became very much as we see it today, a street of fashionable coffee shops, restaurants, taverns and theatres. It has always fascinated writers. Virginia Woolf for one was struck by its character – she writes in *Mrs Dalloway* (1925) that the Strand was 'quite different from Westminster', being 'so serious; it was so busy'; John Masefield, in his poem 'Growing Old' writes of 'jostling in the Strand'.

Hereabouts, if we are playing the Great Game, is the location of the 'worn and battered tin dispatch box' entrusted to Watson's bank, Cox and Co, which contains many adventures not as yet released to the public. This would be the Holy Grail for Sherlockians and many are the pastiches – new tales of Holmes – that begin by pretending that the author has somehow come by the mystical box. From 1888 the HQ of Cox and Co. was at the junction of Trafalgar Square and the Strand, 16–18 Charing Cross, subsequently moving to Pall Mall.

'To walk alone in London is the greatest rest.'

Virginia Woolf, 1930

As already mentioned, Watson stayed at a private hotel in the Strand when he first returned to England from his military service. There used to be a large hotel called the Golden Cross Hotel just before reaching Charing Cross station where rooms could be had for considerably less than the Northumberland Avenue establishments and it is thought by many that Watson could have stayed here.

It is interesting to note that this area already had an impeccable literary pedigree; almost fifty years earlier, Charles Dickens placed the adult David Copperfield and his Aunt Betsy in a similar location. In fact, the whole of this area – Embankment, Villiers Street, the Strand and Covent Garden – were Copperfield's world as a youngster growing up while his father was imprisoned for debt. These events in the novel are largely autobiographical.[24] The hopelessly grim blacking factory to which Copperfield – i.e. Dickens – was sent was where Embankment tube is now; on a happier note, Copperfield tells us that he became an expert in where to buy bread pudding in this area – the 'flabby' sort with currants widely spaced was half the price of his favourite which was much more fruity and could be had in a shop on the Strand – and he would eke out his meagre pay as best he could. Once, he thinks it might have been on his birthday, he had the courage to enter a pub somewhere around here called 'The Lion or The Lion and something', and ask the landlady for a pint of 'your very best ale'. She gave it to him, no doubt considerably diluted, along with a kiss, refusing to take his money.[25]

Charing Cross itself in the front of the station is a copy of a medieval 'cross' (such crosses were granted by the monarch to mark something or somebody special, e.g. Norwich was granted one by King Edward II in 1341 to denote the right to hold an open market in perpetuity, and they were edifices of any shape, rarely in the form of an actual cross) erected in 1291–4 by Edward I as a memorial to his wife, Eleanor of Castile. This was destroyed on the orders of Oliver Cromwell in 1647 and a reimagining of the original, designed by E.M. Barry and made of stone and Aberdeen granite, was erected in 1865.

Both Charing Cross station and Charing Cross Post Office feature in several Holmes adventures. Telegrams from Charing Cross Post Office – actually situated in this period behind where you are walking now, in Trafalgar Square, on what was subsequently the site of South Africa House – feature in *The Hound of the Baskervilles* and *The Adventure of Wisteria Lodge*. As regards the station, Holmes arrives back at Charing Cross accompanied by Hopkins at the successful conclusion of *The Adventure of the Golden Pince-Nez* and in *Scandal in Bohemia* Holmes learns that Irene Adler – *the* woman – has left for the Continent on the 5.15 train from here.

The thrilling end of *The Adventure of the Bruce-Partington Plans* takes place in the smoking room of the Charing Cross Hotel, an enterprise fronting the station itself, still thriving and looking much the same on the outside as in Holmes' day. Oberstein is tricked by a dictated note from Holmes to come to the hotel to collect the final tracing of the plans for £500 and here he is duly arrested before being 'engulphed for fifteen years in a British prison'. In his trunk are located the invaluable Bruce-Partington plans which he had been intending to sell by auction to a rival naval power in Europe. Following this, Holmes spends a day at Windsor whence he returns with a remarkably fine emerald tie-pin saying it was 'a present from a certain gracious lady in whose interests he had once been fortunate enough to carry out a small commission'.

Almost opposite the station is Coutts Bank. This was previously 'the Strand end of the Lowther Arcade', through which, in *The Final Problem*, Watson is directed by Holmes to rush in order to pick up a cab to Victoria Station. Watson does as he is bidden and arrives in the appointed first-class carriage only to find that Holmes does not appear. Instead he is sharing the compartment, which has been reserved for Holmes and himself only, with a decrepit Italian ecclesiastic. The train is about to pull out and Watson feels 'a chill of fear' before hearing a voice, 'My dear Watson, you have not even condescended to say good-morning.' The venerable Italian priest is, of course, Holmes in disguise.

The first scene of *The Adventure of the Missing Three-Quarter* finds Holmes puzzling over a strange telegram: 'Please await me. Terrible misfortune. Right wing three-quarter missing, indispensable to-morrow.' Holmes remarks that it has a Strand postmark and was dispatched at ten thirty-six. Thus begins one of the most unusual of tales. Although we are not told as much, the telegram would have presumably been sent from the Charing Cross Telegraph Office which at the time was situated at 447 Strand, just a few doors from the Lowther Arcade on the same side of the road.

Charing Cross Hospital was, at the time of the Holmes adventures, in Agar Street, just off the Strand on the landward side at this point. At the beginning of *The Hound of the Baskervilles*, Holmes challenges Watson to make what he can of a stick which has been left by a visitor at 221B.

It bears the words 'from his friends of the CCH'. Watson judges this to be of 'the Something Hunt.' In one of the most amusing exchanges in the canon, Holmes tells Watson that he excels himself but unfortunately most of his conclusions are erroneous. Holmes judges it to be 'Charing Cross Hospital' and when the man, Dr James Mortimer, returns he is, of course, proved quite right. His friends had presented it to him when he left the hospital to go into private practice. In *The Adventure of the Illustrious Client*, Holmes is attacked by two men and escapes through the Café Royal into Glasshouse Street. He is carried to Charing Cross Hospital and then insists on returning to Baker Street (see above where a severely shaken Watson reads the newspaper report of this frightening occurrence in Northumberland Avenue).

Both Conan Doyle and Charles Dickens knew the Strand very well, featured it in their writings and also put on plays here with considerable financial success.[26] One of the most remarkable for Conan Doyle was *The Speckled Band* which was premiered at the Adelphi, still thriving today and on the left as you now look up the Strand, on 10 June 1910. Conan Doyle writes that it was a very quick job – two weeks, in fact, was all it took to convert the story – and this was necessary because his previous play at the venue, *The House of Temperley*, had been forced to close despite financial success, as a mark of respect, agreed by all west End producers, on the death of King Edward VII. This in effect ended the play's run. Conan Doyle, however, having leased the theatre could not afford to have it standing empty, and luckily the new play quickly made up any losses – when full, the theatre could house 1,500 people plus another 500 standing and a successful season could enrich all concerned very quickly. He writes that he purchased a live snake for the production – 'the pride of my heart', he says in *Memories and Adventures* – a feature not appreciated by all critics, one of whom wrote that it was 'a palpably artificial serpent'; Conan Doyle was tempted to offer the critic a good sum of money to go to bed with it.

The real problem with the hastily written play, according to Conan Doyle, was that in trying to give Holmes a worthy adversary, he managed to produce a more interesting character in the villain. He also considered the ending terrible. Neither of these things, however, prevented the play being a runaway financial success.

Other Conan Doyle theatrical productions

Conan Doyle considered *Fires of Fate* (1909 initially at the Lyric in London) to be his best theatrical work. It starred Lewis Waller and it is adapted from the story *The Tragedy of Korosko* (1897). Conan Doyle remarked that he loved to sit and watch the audience responding to the play and that there was really nothing like this in the life of a book writer. However, its relative failure was a disappointment. A silent film was made with the same title in 1923.

His other dramatic venture was *Brigadier Gerard* (performed between March and June 1906 at the Imperial and Lyric Theatres, London) and which he described as 'mildly successful'. Once again it starred Lewis Waller, his performance being described by Conan Doyle as 'glorious'. The brand-new uniforms of chestnut and silver cost over £100 and when the author saw them during dress rehearsal he was appalled because the soldiers were meant to have been out for months in all weathers. He said that the men were warriors, not ballet dancers and he covered the uniforms in mud and dust and tore holes in them – all except that of Waller who insisted on maintaining his immaculate appearance during performances. Conan Doyle was a great fan of the man, and writes that he once came down to *Windlesham* where, reciting in the music room, his clear resonant voice made the glass lampshades on the wall tremble. Waller died prematurely of pneumonia in 1915, Conan Doyle remembering him as 'a very wonderful man'.

Walking on from the Adelphi you will soon see, on the other side of the road, one of London's legendary hotels: The Savoy, the gilded entrance tucked back from the main thoroughfare in its own private street. It is the only luxury hotel on the River Thames. Edward VII, Charlie Chaplin, Noel Coward, Frank Sinatra, Oscar Wilde, Harry Truman, Bob Dylan and many others of the world's rich and famous have stayed here. Winston Churchill liked to bring his cabinet colleagues here for lunch.

A little farther along is Simpson's in the Strand. Conan Doyle and Dickens were regulars here at the peak of their respective careers. Not surprisingly, therefore, this was also a favourite restaurant of Holmes and Watson with Simpson's own website proudly pointing out that at the end of *The Adventure of the Dying Detective*, Holmes, after fasting for three days, tells Watson 'something nutritious at Simpson's would not be out of place'. Also, in *The Adventure of the Illustrious Client*, Watson meets up with his friend one evening at Simpson's to discuss the case. A short while later in the same story, Watson writes that they once more dined here.

Burleigh Street branches off the northern side of the Strand a short distance along from Simpson's. This was the original home of *The Strand Magazine* which ran to 711 issues from 1891 to 1950. It was the first to publish the Sherlock Holmes stories and settled down at sales of about 500,000 copies an issue for several decades up to the 1930s. In all, Conan Doyle provided the magazine with 121 short stories and nine novels. During serialisation of *The Hound of the Baskervilles*, people queued up outside the offices, impatient for the next instalment. It also published the Raffles series, written by Conan Doyle's brother-in-law, E.W. Hornung; these stories are discussed in detail in Walk 6.

On a few occasions, in investigating Holmes' activities, some mild detective work of our own is needed. Here is one such. Soon, as the walk continues straight along the Strand and past Waterloo Bridge on your right, you will come to the magnificent Somerset House and it is here that Holmes presumably checked out the details of Mrs Stoner's will in *The Adventure of the Speckled Band*. Holmes told Watson that he was going to 'Doctors' Commons' – which used to house wills and is lampooned by Dickens in *David Copperfield* as 'a cosy, dosey, old-fashioned, time-forgotten, sleepy-headed little family party', and was based at Paternoster Row near St Paul's – but this had been closed down in 1867 and wills transferred to Somerset House; *The Adventure of the Speckled Band* is set in 1883.

Soon the Strand becomes Fleet Street. Holmes and Watson would walk these streets not just on business but also for pleasure. At the beginning of *The Resident Patient*, Watson writes that Holmes suggests a ramble through London: 'I was weary of our little sitting room and gladly acquiesced. For three hours we strolled about together, watching the ever-changing kaleidoscope of life as it ebbs and flows through Fleet Street and the Strand'. It was ten before they returned to Baker Street.

Ye Old Cheddar Cheese is a small pub at 145 Fleet Street, on the left-hand side as you walk. It has been frequented by many literary figures, including Dickens, Conan Doyle and probably once or twice – he is reputed to have forsworn alcohol in his later years, preferring tea – by Dr Johnson who lived just behind it in Gough Square where he completed his famous Dictionary in 1755. Nip up the alleyway at the side of the pub, Wine Office Court, to take a look at this and some of Dr Johnson's 'innumerable little lanes and courts'. A sign on the side wall of the pub claims that some of the people who came either in search of Dr Johnson or the pub itself include Voltaire, Congreve, Pope, Tennyson, Boswell, Macaulay, Thackeray, Wilkie Collins, Theodore Roosevelt, Mark Twain, Chesterton, Yeats and a host of others.

It has been claimed by some that the headquarters of *The Red-headed League*, which Conan Doyle gives as 7 Pope's Court, was in one of the little alleyways at the back of 'The Cheese'; others consider Poppins Court, a little farther up Fleet Street on the same side of the road, to have been more likely. In this story, all red-headed men who were looking for a job at a salary of £4 a week 'for purely nominal services' were asked to report here to a Mr Duncan Ross at eleven o'clock on a Monday. It turns out to be a highly creative attempt at mischief by a villain named John Clay and at the end of the story Holmes expresses his admiration for a man whose mind could come up with something like this (although, of course, regretting that such a mind is devoted to crime).

One thing we know as fact from the *Guardian* newspaper is that on 5 October 1926, Sir Arthur Conan Doyle was a guest speaker here, at the beginning of the Pudding Season at the pub, for a very convivial evening in honour of Dr Johnson. The newspaper reports that Lord Birkenhead spoke first and then Sir Arthur, who said that Dr Johnson was a great man but a poor writer; his English was fit for tombstones, not for books – and no one read his books. This was disputed by the next speaker, Mr Birrell.

The walk continues through Ludgate Hill to St Paul's Cathedral. St Paul's has been on this site for 1,400 years and has been built and rebuilt five times. The task of designing the present structure was assigned to Sir Christopher Wren in 1669 – he had already begun the task of replacing over fifty churches destroyed in the Great Fire of London in 1666. It was consecrated on 16 December 1697.

Returning to the story of *The Red-headed League*, it was at '17 King Edward Street, near St Paul's' that the affronted Mr Jabez Wilson seeks in vain for the offices of his supposed employers but finds at the address 'a manufactory of artificial kneecaps'. Also, in the final stages of *The Sign of Four,* as Holmes, Watson and Jones track down the *Aurora* along the River Thames past St Paul's, we find Watson in poetic mode: 'As we passed the City, the last rays of the sun were gilding the cross on the summit of St Paul's.' Well, maybe this is because he was in love with Miss Mary Morstan by now, 'as truly as ever a man loved a woman', which in the story he is to tell her shortly.

One last stop on this walk could be St Paul's Wharf, which some believe to be the site of The Bar of Gold in *The Man with the Twisted Lip*, an opium den, 'the vilest murder-trap on the whole riverside'. Alternatively, this could be farther along the river, near London Bridge; that it is on the east side is generally agreed but Sherlockians have not been able to agree more. One thought is that it is a disguised name for various similar locations. Victorian and early twentieth-century authors, such as Dickens,[27] Wilkie Collins and Conan Doyle, were much given to contrasting the domestic bliss and comforts of a middle-class home with the terrors, filth and degradation that were merely a short cab ride, or small addictive habit, away.

A further item of interest about this tale is that it contains one of Conan Doyle's mistakes, probably caused by the rapidity with which it was written: at the beginning of the tale Mrs Watson refers to her husband as 'James' and not 'John'.

The first silent film version of this tale was in 1921.

WALK 3

London: Walking along Oxford Street, Regent Street, around Piccadilly Circus and into Haymarket

At A Glance – the following stories, plays and novels are highlighted in this walk:

The Adventure of the Three Garridebs. The Adventure of the Empty House. The Hound of the Baskervilles. The Adventure of Charles Augustus Milverton. The Adventure of the Blue Carbuncle. The Final Problem. The Disappearance of Lady Frances Carfax. The Resident Patient. The Adventure of the Noble Bachelor. The Adventure of the Three Gables. The Problem of Thor Bridge. His Last Bow. The Adventure of the Illustrious Client. A Scandal in Bohemia. The Red-headed League. A Study in Scarlet. The Greek Interpreter. The Adventure of the Retired Colourman

Distance: About 3.9 kilometres/2.5 miles

Time to allow: A complete day for the walking: at the end in the Haymarket/Leicester Square area there are pubs, clubs, cinemas, theatres and restaurants.

Walking conditions: You will be walking along the busiest shopping streets in London – Oxford Street and Regent Street – and into the tourist hot-spots of Piccadilly Circus and Haymarket. Public seating is very limited but there are dozens of places to buy a drink or meal. The route is mainly flat. As ever, take a camera!

Route
- Marble Arch tube station
- Connaught Place
- Park Lane
- Oxford Street
- Brook Street
- Regent Street
- Hanover Square
- Conduit Street
- Piccadilly Circus
- Haymarket

This walk begins at Marble Arch – Marble Arch tube station is on the Central (red) line. Marble Arch, immediately outside, was designed by John Nash in 1827 and he based it on the Arch of Constantine in Rome. Originally designed as the gateway to Buckingham Palace (only members of the Royal Family could pass through the arches) it was moved – some say 'relegated' – to where it is now, in the middle of a roaring roundabout, in 1857. A series of subways will take you from the tube station to the arch and then on to Speakers Corner, Hyde Park and Park Lane.

This specific part of London was where criminals would be hanged. Almost opposite, at the end of North Carriage Drive, was the area where once soldiers would be shot for cowardice. Conan Doyle refers to the Tyburn Tree, a tablet at the location of the hangings which you will see set in the pavement if you visit the home of Nathan Garrideb as given below. The first recorded execution was in 1196, and from 1571 a three-sided gallows was erected here. This enabled mass-hangings such as that in June 1649 when twenty-three men and one woman were hanged simultaneously. Those sentenced to the gallows would often be brought in open carts from St Giles, some drinking heavily if they had been able to bribe their gaolers, along the length of Oxford Street, in front of cheering, leering crowds. Once at Tyburn, they were sometimes allowed a last speech at a place that became known as Speakers' Corner.

The last public execution, of John Austin, a highwayman, took place at Tyburn on 3 November 1783. Speakers' Corner, however, still flourishes and on Sunday mornings, anyone can go there (some literally bringing a box to stand on) and talk about anything whatsoever provided it does not lead to a breach of the peace. This is a very entertaining, even sometimes informative but more often a little crazy, spectacle for Londoners and visitors alike.

The first literary stop on this walk is to the home of Nathan Garrideb. We learn that this adventure took place at the latter end of June 1902 – Watson was able to be specific on this point as it was the previous month that Holmes had refused a knighthood, the circumstances of which are kept secret from the reader as Watson does not wish to commit any indiscretion. In this wonderful tale, *The Adventure of the Three Garridebs*, Nathan Garrideb's address is given as 136 Little Ryder Street, W. There is no such Street, but Sherlockians point to the house and street details as perfectly fitting Connaught Place, a few minutes stroll from Marble Arch tube station; turn right out of the station, and right again into Edgeware Road. An alleyway leading to Connaught Place leads off the street on your left a short distance along.

The return of Holmes

In *The Adventure of the Empty House*, the Oxford Street end of Park Lane marks the spot where Watson and Holmes reunite, albeit unbeknown to Watson and only for a few brief seconds. The year is 1894 and Holmes had been gone three years. Watson, now a widower, wanders across Hyde Park and, fascinated by the recent unsolved murder of the young Honourable Ronald Adair in a locked room at 427 Park Lane, finds himself outside the house, trying to apply the methods of Sherlock Holmes to solve the crime. To the reader, his hopelessness, and that of the police when faced with a seemingly impossible crime, brings home just how lost the world is without Sherlock Holmes, who would surely have solved the case. Watson accidentally bumps into an elderly deformed man who drops some books which he is carrying. Watson helps pick them up, mumbles apologies and returns to his home in Kensington. The man reappears there, reveals that he is Holmes and is indeed not dead, and Watson faints for the first and last time in his life.[28] Holmes is back.

Oxford Street and the stories

The walk resumes from Marble Arch tube station and down Oxford Street, which claims to be Europe's busiest shopping street with over half a million visitors daily. Originally a Roman road through the city, the fields in this area started to be bought up by the Earl of Oxford in the eighteenth century. Until this time, it had not been seen as a desirable place for home or business with public hangings at one end and the notorious St Giles slums at the other. It was redesigned in conjunction with Regent Street by John Nash from 1810.

As far as the Holmes stories are concerned, Oxford Street features in part as a road along which people rush to get somewhere else, are tracked or followed, and cabs clatter. In *The Hound of the Baskervilles*, Holmes and Watson follow Sir Henry Baskerville and Dr Mortimer, unbeknown to them and keeping 200 yards behind, from Baker Street 'into Oxford Street and so down Regent Street'. During the early stages of *The Adventure of Charles Augustus Milverton*, Holmes picks up a cab in Oxford Street to drive to Hampstead. At the end of the tale Holmes jumps to his feet. 'Take your hat! Come with me!' he says to Watson and rushes 'at his top speed down Baker Street and along Oxford Street until we almost reached Regent's Circus'. Here they find a shop, the windows of which are filled with the beauties and celebrities of the day including a stately lady they have recently seen performing an act of vengeance and Holmes, acting as both judge and jury, not for the first time, regards the case as closed. Looking at Watson he puts his finger to his lips and they turn away from the window.

In *The Adventure of the Blue Carbuncle*, a goose is the central feature and Watson reports that, as they go in search of the said bird's origin, 'our footfalls rang crisp and loudly', and he and Holmes travel through 'Wimpole Street, Harley Street and so through Wigmore Street into Oxford Street.' Also, Holmes is certain in *The Final Problem* that Moriarty is at the root of the affair when: 'I went out about midday to transact some business in Oxford Street. As I passed the corner which leads from Bentinck Street on to the Welbeck Street crossing a two-horse van furiously driven whizzed round and was on me like a flash...'

There are specific points of interest along Oxford Street. Two relate to where Holmes and Watson shop. Bradley, supplier of Holmes' 'strongest shag' – liable to reduce the air in the front room of 221B to an almost unbreathable fug – is here, as is Latimer's, where Watson buys his boots. Watson mentions this at the very start of *The Disappearance of Lady Frances Carfax*. Holmes is then able to deduce, just from the way the laces on his nearly new boots are tied, that Watson has been for a Turkish Bath.

The streets immediately to the south are very well represented also. In *Silver Blaze* we hear of a milliner's account for £37 15s made out by Madame Lesurier of Bond Street. On another occasion in *The Hound of the Baskervilles*, once the bright young lad, Cartwright, has been dispatched around the twenty-three hotels in the immediate vicinity of Charing Cross to search for the centre page of the *Times* with some parts cut from it with scissors, Holmes proposes that he and Watson pass some time at one of the Bond Street galleries. In *The Resident Patient* Holmes is informed that Dr Percy Trevelyan lives at 403 Brook Street (this highly fashionable street runs parallel to Oxford Street, from Park Lane to Regent Street). Then, Lord St Simon writes to Holmes from Grosvenor Mansions in *The Adventure of the Noble Bachelor*, and in *The Adventure of the Three Gables*, Holmes and Watson take a cab to Grosvenor Square.

Claridge's Hotel, Brook Street, which once entertained Queen Victoria and was opened in 1856, features in the stories, notably The *Problem of Thor Bridge* – J. Neil Gibson sends a letter to Holmes from the hotel asking for his help in proving Miss Dunbar's innocence. It also has the distinction of being the only hotel in central London in which it can be proved from the text (as opposed to what many enthusiasts, when playing the Great Game, surmise) that Holmes ever stayed; at the end of *His Last Bow* Holmes tells Martha that she can report to him at Claridge's and confirms he will be returning there. Some readers like to think that Martha is Mrs Hudson from 221B, but the way Holmes addresses the old lady, in a fairly reserved fashion, leaves doubts and surely Watson would have greeted her more effusively had she been his old housekeeper? It is interesting that in the wonderful Russian TV series *The Adventures of Sherlock Holmes and Dr Watson*, starring Vasily Livanov as Holmes, it is made quite clear that Martha *is* Mrs Hudson. Did Watson also stay at Claridge's? Some Sherlockians are convinced that he would have accompanied Holmes for at least a short break before confronting the horrors of the Great War, especially so as Holmes had in his pocket a cheque for £500 that he was eager to cash before it was stopped by the drawer. The story presents some further unanswered questions, in particular, why does it read more like a James Bond spy story than a traditional Holmes adventure? And why is it written in the third person? *His Last Bow* was published in 1917 and it is possible that Conan Doyle changed his approach in order to better write a story that he considered would raise morale during the hostilities.

As a collection, *His Last Bow* was banned for a period in 1923 in some Dundee schools after a Highland Minister picked up a copy in a school and reported to the education committee that it was no less than a text book to teach boys to rob and murder.

Regent Street

This walk turns right down Regent Street at Oxford Circus – Oxford Street continues straight on with some interesting Holmes locations nearer the Tottenham Court Road end and these are covered in Walk 4.

Regent Street was designed by John Nash and James Burton from 1811 and redesigned near the end of the century. It was originally to have been straight, to look triumphal, but land ownership issues resulted in its now famous curved shape. No residential accommodation was built above the shops which led a strangely deserted air to it when business was done. One idea at the time was that the street would act as a divide between the upper classes in Mayfair and the lower classes in Soho. Much of it has always been owned by the Crown Estate on behalf of the monarch, although some parts were sold off in the 1970s to finance regeneration.

Hanover Square is a pleasant leafy oasis in which to take a rest or eat a snack – there are seats – and is the first stop as we head down Regent Street, turning right at Princes Street. St George's Hanover Square church is a short distance to the south of the square and the location of Lord St Simon's proposed marriage to American Hatty Doran, only to have her run away during the wedding breakfast in *The Adventure of the Noble Bachelor*. It was built in 1721–5, designed by John James and has an impressive portico supported by six Corinthian columns which extends out over the pavement. Land being very scarce, it was constructed without a graveyard and people in the parish, which included Laurence Sterne (1716–68), author of *Tristram Shandy*, were buried in the grounds of the nearby workhouse.[29] It rapidly became a fashionable wedding church, one of them being that of Theodore Roosevelt, aged 28, and Edith Carrow, aged 25, on 2 December 1886. In popular culture, the church in the song 'Get me to the church on time' from *My Fair Lady* is St George's.

A few yards south is Conduit Street, the home of Colonel Sebastian Moran, second only to Moriarty in the hierarchy of crime; Conan Doyle gives us his own take on the most dangerous men in the stories but all readers will probably have their own cherished opinion. We learn of his street address (but not the number) in *The Adventure of the Empty House*. He is, according to Holmes' index of biographies, the son of Sir Augustus Moran C.B., educated at Eton and Cambridge, a most distinguished soldier, author of two books on hunting and life in the jungle, and 'the best heavy-game shot that our Eastern Empire ever produced'.

Colonel Sebastian Moran is mentioned in *The Adventure of the Illustrious Client* and *His Last Bow* but it is in *The Adventure of the Empty House* that the reader gains a detailed sense of the man.[30] He is someone who has gained high honour in battle and the grateful thanks of his queen and country, and yet cheats at cards. His criminal exploits, including the 'impossible' shooting of young Adair and his plans for the death of Holmes are very creative and require an iron nerve, yet he fails to adequately reconnoitre the scene of his most audacious crime to date (the proposed murder of Holmes himself). After being outwitted by Holmes with the help of Watson and Lestrade, all he can mutter is, 'you cunning, cunning fiend'. Later, Watson expresses surprise that a man so distinguished, should revert to evil ways. 'There are some trees, Watson,' says Holmes, 'which grow to a certain height, and then develop some unsightly eccentricity. You will see it often in humans.' The story is remarkable for having Mrs Hudson play a key role, unquestionably endangering her own life, only to have Holmes peremptorily thank and dismiss her at the end. Holmes is sometimes accused of being cold and inhuman and Jeremy Brett, many people's favourite Holmes, once said that he disliked the arrogance of the man.

Conan Doyle and soldiering

The mentions of Moran's military distinctions apart, there is very little of soldiering in the tales. This is opposed to Conan Doyle's own life where nothing, not even Sherlock Holmes, had a more profound impact.

Conan Doyle described the routine life of a private soldier as a delightful one – cleaning this and that, keeping his rifle in good order, being led and not leading. One amusing incident involved a new adjutant arriving and reviewing his section. Conan Doyle describes him as a cocky little fellow, who in age could have been his son. Having exchanged a few words with Conan Doyle the adjutant asked the CO who the big fellow was that he had been talking to. 'That's Sherlock Holmes,' he said. 'Good Lord!' said the adjutant.

His immediate and extended family suffered terribly in the Great War. The first to die was Malcolm Leckie, his wife's brother. Then Miss Loder Symonds, who lived with the family, lost three of her brothers and the fourth was wounded before she herself passed on. Two nephews, Alec Forbes and Oscar Hornung, then perished. A sniper killed his brother-in-law, Major Oldham, in the trenches. Finally a double blow: firstly his son Kingsley, 'one of the grandest boys in body and soul that ever a father was blessed with', who was badly wounded at the Somme and carried off with pneumonia in London; thereafter Innes, his brother and companion of the youthful days in Southsea, died from the same disease. Conan Doyle subsequently said it was a source of the utmost solace that, of all these, there was only one whose posthumous existence he could not to his satisfaction subsequently establish through his practice of spiritualism.

Conduit Street leads directly back to Regent Street where the walk continues towards Piccadilly. In *A Scandal in Bohemia*, Godfrey Norton instructs a cabby to 'drive like the devil' to Gross and Hankey's in Regent Street before going on to St Monica's church in the Edgeware Road (fictional) where he is to marry Irene Adler; we are not told but presumably this is to buy a wedding ring.

On the left-hand side, not far from the Eros statue in Piccadilly, is the Café Royal. In the 1890s this was already a famous meeting place for the great and the good of the day including George Bernard Shaw, Max Beerbohm and Oscar Wilde, who famously met his friend Frank Harris here on 24 March 1895 to discuss what to do about Lord Alfred Douglas' father, the Marquess of Queensbury, against whom Wilde had issued a charge of criminal libel.[31] It is outside the café that Holmes was set upon in *The Adventure of the Illustrious Client* and escaped through the café into Glasshouse Street; he was, however, injured badly enough to need medical assistance from Charing Cross Hospital before returning to Baker Street.

Between the Quadrant in Regent Street and Piccadilly, Vine Street and George Court lay St James's Hall; opened in 1858 and capable of sitting, in the main hall (there were two more smaller theatres) over 2,000, it became the most popular concert hall in London. Holmes relaxes here during a quiet lull during the untangling of events in *The Red-headed League*. Watson paints an unusual picture of this side of Holmes 'sat in the stalls wrapped in the most perfect happiness', with 'his gently smiling face, and languid dreamy eyes', the opposite of the 'sleuth-hound' (the reader may wonder during this very detailed description whether Watson is paying attention to the concert – German music rather than Italian or French, according to Holmes when planning the trip – at all, but the truth is probably that he found his famous friend far more interesting) and concludes that 'an evil time' may be coming to those Holmes was engaged in hunting down.

The tale is additionally interesting because it mentions a vegetarian restaurant. 'There is Mortimer's, the tobacconist, the little newspaper shop, the Coburg branch of the City and suburban Bank, the Vegetarian Restaurant and McFarlane's carriage-building depot.' Although Vegetarian food is associated in part with the Jains in India 2,500 years ago, and ancient Greece to some extent, fashionable vegetarian restaurants in England only came into existence at about this time; thus this one, noticed by Holmes, must have been one of the very first.

In Piccadilly Circus itself is the Criterion Restaurant, opened in 1874. It is here in *A Study in Scarlet* that Watson met young Stamford and mentioned that he was looking for affordable accommodation, which is really the very first scene in the adventures themselves.

There are a couple more points of interest in this area before this walk ends. The first is Charing Cross which is where Mr Melas, in *The Greek*

Interpreter, starts to become concerned that this route, which carries on up the Shaftesbury Avenue, is an odd way to Kensington and says as much. His fellow traveller responds by pulling down the carriage blinds and producing 'a formidable-looking bludgeon loaded with lead'. The second is the Haymarket Theatre which is where old Josiah Amberley, in *The Adventure of the Retired Colourman*, claims to have bought two tickets as a treat for his wife in the upper circle; at the last moment, however, she claimed a headache and could not go. Amberley said he had gone alone. Watson, however, had seen and remembered the number of 'her' ticket, from which Holmes is able to prove that Amberley is a liar as neither of the seats either side had been occupied during the performance in question.

You are now in the very centre of one of the prime tourist areas of London – Piccadilly Circus, Trafalgar Square and Leicester Square with, practically speaking, a never-ending array of restaurants, take-away outlets, cinemas, theatres, galleries and pubs. As already mentioned, there is a half-price theatre ticket kiosk in Leicester Square – always worth a try. Trafalgar Square is discussed in detail in Walk 6.

Walk 1

Travelling to Baker Street is easy by underground train (tube) – see text. Alternatively, travel from virtually anywhere central – Trafalgar Square, Charing Cross etc – to the Baker Street area, where this walk begins, by bus. In this picture, one of the New Routemasters is making its way to north London past the St Pancras Renaissance London Hotel.

Sherlock Holmes statue by John Doubleday, immediately outside Baker Street station. It can speak to you (see text).

Plaques on Chiltern Court, on the right-hand side as you enter Baker Street from Marylebone Road.

Sherlock Holmes Museum: best to arrive as early as possible for quicker entry (opens at 0930 hrs).

2 Upper Wimpole Street.

Walk 2

Northumberland Avenue is a wide, leafy thoroughfare.

The well-known Sherlock Holmes pub.

Charing Cross Station now does not look very different to Holmes' day when it was the scene for the coup de grâce in *The Adventure of the Bruce-Partington Plans*.

The Strand: Holmes and Watson knew this grand street very well and it features in a number of stories (see text).

The Adelphi today – the scene of theatrical and financial triumph for Conan Doyle (as it had been for Dickens before him).

Simpson's – Holmes and Watson dined here sometimes, as in *The Adventure of the Illustrious Client*.

The Strand leads into Fleet Street which in Holmes' time was the headquarters of major newspapers and magazines.

'The Cheese' was known to many literary greats through the centuries, including Conan Doyle who spoke here to honour Dr Johnson in October 1926 (see text).

Could Pope's Court – *The Red-headed League* – have been an alley around here?

St Paul's Cathedral rises magnificently over Ludgate Hill at the end of this walk: 'the last rays of the sun were gilding the cross on the summit of St Paul's' (*The Sign of Four*).

Walk 3

'...and found myself at about six o'clock at the Oxford Street end of Park Lane'. In *The Adventure of the Empty House*, Watson stood here as he contemplated the shooting of young Ronald Adair and bumped into an elderly, deformed man who dropped some books. (*Photograph by Daniel Tink*)

This is the bar in Piccadilly, now a restaurant, where Watson dropped in for a drink while looking in vain for affordable London accommodation. Here, he met young Stamford who suggested meeting another friend of his who was also looking for a flat-share – the friend happened to be Sherlock Holmes.

The famous statue in Piccadilly commonly known as Eros – actually called the Shaftesbury Memorial Fountain – and designed by Alfred Gilbert which is close to the Café Royal where Holmes was set upon in *The Adventure of the Illustrious Client*.

Walk 4

Tottenham Court Road, as you step out of the tube today, is a bustling area with theatres, offices and high-end shops. It was less grand in Holmes' day, but still very busy, and the scene of dramatic happenings at the beginning of *The Adventure of the Blue Carbuncle*.

The British Museum. Holmes had rooms in Montague Street, just round the corner from the British Museum when he first came up to London. Mr Henry Baker in *The Adventure of the Blue Carbuncle* is to be found there during the day and several characters in other stories live close by. Holmes spends a morning researching in the museum during *The Adventure of Wisteria Lodge*.

Covent Garden has been used by many writers both as a place to live and in their works (see text). Holmes and Watson go looking for a goose here as this area, nowadays filled with tourists eating and drinking, was then a market. It was and is, also, the centre of theatre-land.

The Royal Opera House, where Holmes and Watson rush to catch the Second Act of a Wagner evening in *The Adventure of the Red Circle*.

The imposing frontage of the Lyceum Theatre is where Mary Morstan, Holmes and Watson wait for a mysterious contact in *The Sign of Four*.

Walk 5

Waterloo station plays a small part in several stories and a more dramatic one in *The Five Orange Pips*.

Sir Joseph Bazalgette, whose monument you will see on the left bank as you walk up this Embankment which he designed, was responsible for London's 'cathedral of sewage' which, although invisible underground, helped wipe out cholera in the city and is still in use today.

Walk 6

Pall Mall East leads off from Trafalgar Square – very grand in Sherlock Holmes' day and today. Looking back, you can see the dome of the National Gallery and St Martin-in-the -Fields.

The route passes Green Park and the Ritz Hotel. Holmes and Watson cross this street when going to see Mycroft in the Diogenes Club. Also, although we are not told as much, Watson could have passed here when 'I drove to the London Library in St James's Square' in *The Adventure of the Illustrious Client*.

Heading up to Piccadilly Circus. St James's Hall, where Holmes and Watson go to see Sarasate play in *The Red-headed League*, was on the left-hand side of the street here. On the right hand side, as you reach the statue of Eros, is the Criterion bar where Watson learns about the possibility of a flatshare with another man who turns out to be Sherlock Holmes (see text).

Walk 7

This is the Henry VIII Gatehouse to St Barts. Inside one of the most famous introductions in literature, between Holmes and Watson, took place beginning with the words 'You have been in Afghanistan, I perceive.'

This is near the location of Jabez Wilson's pawnbrokers shop in *The Red-headed League*, at that time a very shabby area but now smart with prestigious office buildings, cafes and interesting pubs.

Entrance to Bank underground line: the walk takes a number of trips to local Holmesian locations from this spot – there are seats here to rest on and plan each venture

The Bank of England: in the BBC production of *Sherlock*, Moriarty accessed the Bank of England, Pentonville prison and The Tower of London on the same day, just to show Holmes that he could. Pastiche writers have enjoyed linking Holmes and the bank together.

The Tower of London features in *The Sign of Four* and is a wonderful location in its own right.

On the way from Cannon Street to Aldgate you can take a trip up to the top of the Monument, built between 1671 and 1677 to commemorate the Great Fire of London, and gain a grand view of this part of London.

Walk 8

The *St Pancras case* is under discussion by Holmes and Watson as *The Adventure of Shoscombe Old Place* begins. The station and hotel alongside were started in 1863 and the completed complex was one of the architectural wonders of the late Victorian period. This is a shot of the Hogwarts-like towers of St Pancras Hotel and seen from the courtyard of the British Library, which moved alongside St Pancras station in 1998 and was the largest public building to be built in twentieth-century Britain.

The Adventure of the Retired Colourman sees Holmes and Watson take a trip to The Royal Albert Hall to hear Carina sing. Six days after Conan Doyle's death a mass séance was held here in the hope of speaking to him (see text).

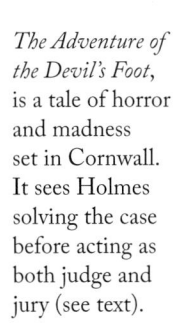

The Adventure of the Devil's Foot, is a tale of horror and madness set in Cornwall. It sees Holmes solving the case before acting as both judge and jury (see text).

Norfolk features in *The 'Gloria Scott'* and Norwich, its capital, in *The Adventure of the Dancing Men*. Conan Doyle liked motoring in the county (see text). This is a panoramic view of the city of Norwich. (*Photograph by Daniel Tink*)

The cliff-tops at Cromer and further up the Norfolk coastline at Beeston Bump (*Photograph by Daniel Tink*) where locals claim that The Black Shuk, a devil dog partial to the throats of any locals foolish enough to roam along the coast at night, was the model for *The Hound of the Baskervilles*.

WALK 4

London: Around Tottenham Court Road and into Holborn and Covent Garden

At A Glance – the following stories, plays and novels are highlighted in this walk:

The Adventure of the Blue Carbuncle. A Case of Identity. The Adventure of the Cardboard Box. The Adventure of the Red Circle. The Musgrave Ritual. The Adventure of the Copper Beeches. The 'Gloria Scott'. The Adventure of the Dancing Men. The Hound of the Baskervilles. The Adventure of Wisteria Lodge. The Adventure of the Retired Colourman. The Man with the Twisted Lip. The Sign of Four

Distance: About 3.5 kilometres/2.2 miles

Time to allow: A morning, afternoon or evening for the basic walking. However, the route encompasses the British Museum, theatreland and Covent Garden with its restaurants and entertainments – usually there are street performers here – so there is really no upper limit on the amount of time to allow.

Walking conditions: Basically flat but some of the streets, such as behind Tottenham Court Road and beside the British Museum, were not originally laid out according to any grand plan and can be a bit of a jumble, which means they can take extra time to navigate especially if there are lots of people about. There are some wonderful photo opportunities, especially around the British Musuem and in Covent Garden.

56   On the Trail of Sherlock Holmes

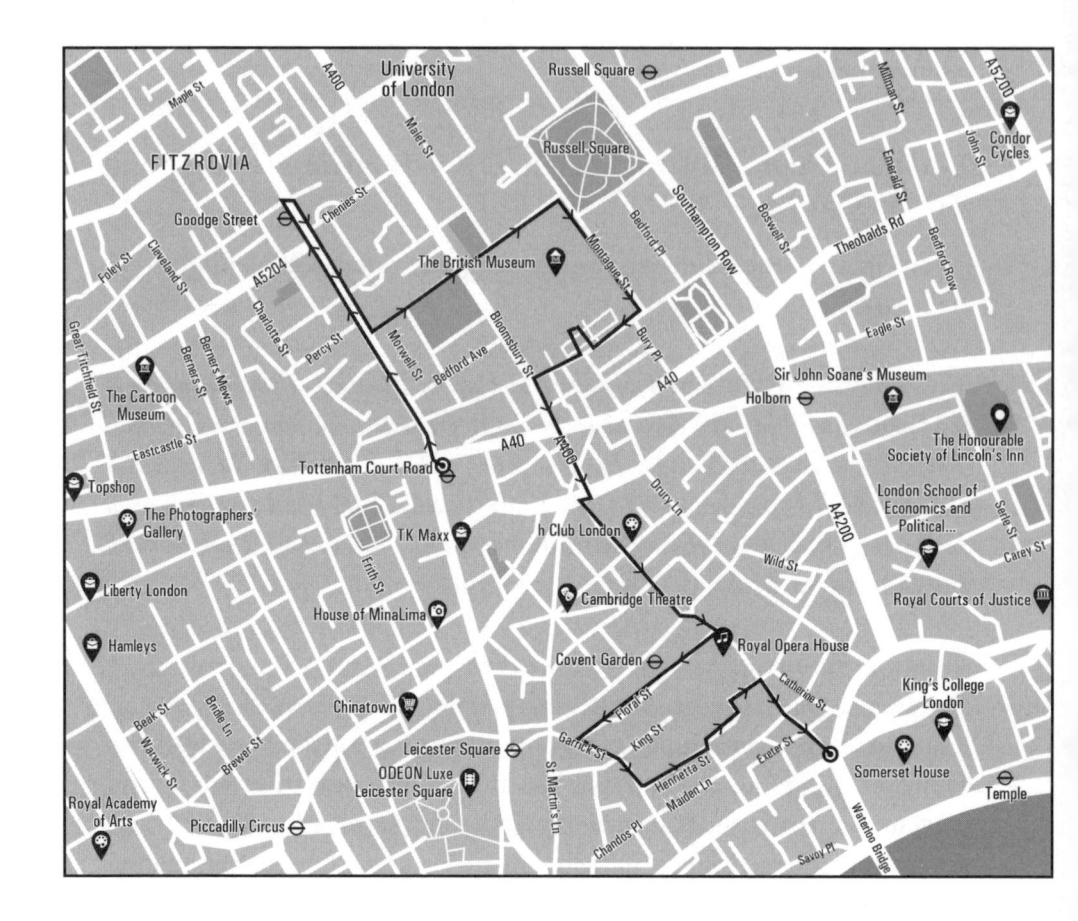

Route
- Tottenham Court Road tube station
- Tottenham Court Road
- Goodge Street
- Bayley Street
- Montague Place
- Russell Square
- Endell Street
- Royal Opera House
- Covent Garden
- Wellington Street

This walk begins at Tottenham Court tube station which is on the Central (red) and Northern (black) lines. Once you could travel from here to the next stop, 'British Museum', but that is closed now. In Conan Doyle's day this was the station for St Giles, a dreadful slum which had been immortalised a few years previously by Charles Dickens in *Bell's Life* where he wrote of 'dirty men, filthy women, squalid children, fluttering shuttlecocks, noisy battledores, reeking pies, bad fruit, more than doubtful oysters, attenuated cats, depressed dogs and anatomical fowls…' It had been through here in the eighteenth century that the carts full of those destined to be hanged would pass, as mentioned in Walk 3.

On leaving the tube, the immediate area is dominated by Centre Point, a 34-storey skyscraper, completed in 1966 and built using pre-cast panels of crushed Portland stone originating in Dorset. Great controversy ensued as it was left empty for nine years because the owner could not secure a tenant for the whole building and refused to let it out floor by floor. In an area of acute homelessness, it became a symbol for many of uncaring capitalism. Now, after many twists and turns, it appears that its fate is to be residential flats and building work on this is ongoing.

Walk along Tottenham Court Road with Centre Point at your back. It is not difficult to imagine being back in 1892 and walking along this street of plumbers, pawnbrokers, locksmiths, grocers and other small businesses. It is around four on Christmas morning and, about half a kilometre along, as you approach Goodge Street on the left, a tallish man looms out of the gaslight. His name, we later learn, is Henry Baker. He has a white goose slung over his shoulder. Staggering slightly as he is a little too full of liquid Christmas cheer, he is accosted by a 'knot of roughs', one of whom knocks off his hat. Raising his stick to defend himself he only succeeds in smashing the shop window behind him. A man dressed in an official-looking commissionaire's uniform who goes by the name of Peterson, an honest fellow well known to the great detective Sherlock Holmes, is fortuitously passing by and runs forward to assist. Baker, however, scared by Peterson – who in the relative gloom resembles a policeman, and fearing arrest for the damage he has caused – drops the goose. He runs as fast as he can towards Oxford Street and vanishes 'in the labyrinth of small streets which lie at the back of Tottenham Court Road'. Thus, thrillingly, begins *The Adventure of the Blue Carbuncle*.

There are three other Holmesian connections to this street:

- In *A Case of Identity*, we learn that businesses here could be worth a tidy penny. Miss Mary Sutherland tells Holmes that her deceased father had been a plumber on Tottenham Court Road. Her mother had remarried and her new husband made her sell the business (as he 'was very superior,

being a traveller in wines') which attracted a price of £4,700 for the goodwill and interest, and this was not even as much as her late lamented father could have secured had he lived and put it up for sale himself.
- In *The Adventure of the Cardboard Box* Holmes regales Watson over dinner with stories about violins including how he had bought a Stradivarius worth at least five hundred guineas for fifty-five shillings from a 'Jew broker's in Tottenham Court Road'.
- Then, during The *Adventure of the Red Circle* Mr Warren, husband of the aggrieved landlady who comes to see Holmes about her unusual tenant, is attacked in the street early in the morning when going to work, and one of the things we learn about him is that he is a timekeeper at Morton and Waylight's in Tottenham Court Road (fictional but it confirms that this is an industrial, as well as a shopping area: there used also to be a major Post Office sorting establishment close to where the tube station is now).

Goodge Street itself is worth a wander down as it contains some interesting eateries and traditional English pubs. Just beyond, on Tottenham Court Road itself, you get a fine view of what is now called BT Tower, a structure 177 metres in height, completed in 1964, and which was a communications tower with a revolving restaurant at the top (one revolution completes every twenty-three minutes). The restaurant was closed in 1980 for security reasons and plans to reopen it in time for the 2012 Olympics came to nothing. It now has an 'Information Band' around the top, the largest of its type in the world with over half a million LEDs.

To continue on this walk, find a point to cross the road and walk back again towards Tottenham Court Road tube. Leading off the main thoroughfare, on your left, you will see Bayley Street which leads straight on to Bedford Square and this becomes Montague Place. As already mentioned in Walk 1, number 23 was where Conan Doyle lived while waiting for non-existent patients in his nearby surgery.

As Conan Doyle knew this area well it is not surprising to find Holmes telling Watson, during the beginning of *The Musgrave Ritual*, that this is where he had rooms when he first came up to London; 'in Montague Street, just round the corner from the British Museum'.[32] They would certainly not have been expensive as Holmes says he had established a 'considerable, though not very lucrative, connection' at this time in his life. Montague Place is also deemed suitable for the lodgings of Violet

Hunter, a young lady seeking employment as a governess, and who describes herself as 'destitute' in *The Adventure of the Copper Beeches*; it is from here that she writes to Holmes seeking an appointment as she has been offered a job at an extraordinary salary of £100 a year. In *The 'Gloria Scott'* Holmes talks of going 'to my London rooms' before his friend, Victor Trevor, pleads with him to return to Donnithorpe in Norfolk; this was, chronologically, his earliest case and so it seems reasonable to assume that he was at the time based at Montague Street, although some scholars believe he may have occupied more than one address during his time in this part of London.

In this location also, 'at the northeast side of the British Museum', is the fictitious Great Orme Street where Conan Doyle placed Mrs Warren's house in *The Adventure of the Red Circle*.

Continuing up Montague Place you will come to Russell Square, which is the location of the boarding house in which Mr Hilton Cubitt stayed in *The Adventure of the Dancing Men*. Here he met and married an American, Elsie Patrick, which led to an intriguing case in the county of Norfolk, further discussed in Chapter 8.

Montague Street leads to a T-junction with Great Russell Street and turning right here will bring you to the main entrance of the British Museum. There are several interesting pubs hereabouts and the pub at which Henry Baker drank and contributed to a goose club in *The Adventure of the Blue Carbuncle* is in this location – we know it is small, on a corner of one of the streets running down into Holborn and was called the Alpha Inn, but that is all. Trying to locate it can be fun and an excellent reason to try some of the local ales and food.

Henry Baker himself spends his days at the British Museum which was founded in 1753, principally comprising the collections of Sir Hans Sloane. It now has over 8 million works, many acquired during the expansion of the British Empire. The Natural History Museum was formed as a branch institution in 1881, the British Library, which is estimated to have between 170 and 200 million items, moving to its own site in 1998. The ownership of some objects, such as the Parthenon Marbles, especially at the time of writing, is disputed. It is one of the greatest museums in the world, an essential visit for everyone, and is currently free to enter although a donation of £5 is encouraged; some parts and exhibition areas may levy a charge if you wish to include these in your visit. It is open every day 10.00am to 5.30pm with a late night on Fridays until 20.30. (www.britishmuseum.org)

The British Museum is especially important four times in the canon. The first, mentioned above, was when Holmes first acquires lodgings 'just round the corner', and we learn that 'there I waited, filling in my too abundant leisure time by studying all those branches of science which might make me more efficient'. Some scholars say that this sentence does not mean that this knowledge was actually gained in the British Museum but it does seem quite probable. The second is in *The Hound of the Baskervilles* where Holmes tells Watson that he had established from the Museum that Stapleton, under the name of Vandeleur, was a recognised authority on entomology and that a moth had been named after Vandeleur as he was the first to describe it. The third is in the summing up for Watson's benefit 'over an evening pipe' in *The Adventure of Wisteria Lodge*, when he says that he spent a morning at the museum reading Eckermann's *Voodooism and the Negroid Religions*.[33] The fourth is in *The Adventure of the Blue Carbuncle* when Mr Henry Baker says that he is to be found there during the day and sometimes frequents the Alpha Inn of an evening.

In *The Adventure of the Blue Carbuncle* Holmes and Watson visit the Alpha Inn, as mentioned above, learn that the goose they are interested in was bought from a salesman in Covent Garden and then 'passed across Holborn, down Endell Street and so through a zigzag of slums to Covent Garden Market'. This walk takes the same basic route, although there are no longer any slums and the market site now consists of restaurants, high-end shops, bars and a large entertainment space.

This is theatreland; the walk passes the magnificent Royal Opera House, sometimes referred to as 'Covent Garden'. It is the third theatre on the site as a result of disastrous fires, with the present building being the result of a comprehensive refurbishment in the 1990s. At the end of *The Adventure of the Red Circle*, Holmes says enthusiastically: 'By the way, it is not yet eight o'clock, and a Wagner night at the opera, Covent Garden. If we hurry, we might be in time for the second act.'

Just before reaching the Royal Opera House, on the other side of the road, is the site of Bow Street Police Station (identifiable today although it closed for good in 1992). It is here, towards the end of *The Man with the Twisted Lip* that Holmes arrives, is greeted cordially by the police on duty, and produces a 'very large bath-sponge' from a Gladstone bag which he proceeds to wet and wash over a very dirty prisoner, smearing away his disguise... 'Let me introduce you,' he exclaimed, 'to Mr Neville St Clair, of Lee, in the county of Kent.' One of the great joys of reading the stories is that Holmes can never resist a dramatic flourish.

Covent Garden had been used since the seventh century as arable land but from 1654 a fruit and vegetable market took hold, followed by houses, taverns and brothels. Parliament took steps to control the area by legislation from the 1830s, leading to a huge growth in the market. By the 1970s traffic congestion was so great that the market relocated to Nine Elms and the area was developed as we see it today. Other attractions, such as the London Transport Museum, were added close by. The buildings are controlled by the Covent Garden Area Trust who pay a peppercorn rent for each lease of one red apple and a posy of flowers. Visitors find it an interesting place to linger, maybe for a drink and a bite, with some just sitting along the street curbs and watching the often-incredible street performers.

Covent Garden and writers

Many writers have used the area in their works or found inspiration here. Samuel Pepys mentions Covent Garden in his famous diaries when, in May 1692, he makes the first mention in literature of a Punch and Judy show. Dr Samuel Johnson reputedly met James Boswell for the first time in a book shop in Covent Garden in 1763. Jane Austen stayed at an apartment here in 1813–14. Thomas de Quincy was living at 36 Tavistock Square, Covent Garden, when he wrote *Confessions of an English Opium-Eater*, published anonymously in 1821. The central figure in George Bernard Shaw's *Pygmalion*, Eliza Doolittle, sells flowers at a market stall. This was, of course, later turned into the famous musical *My Fair Lady*, starring Audrey Hepburn and Sir Rex Harrison.

Charles Dickens has David buy flowers for Dora from the market in *David Copperfield*, while Tom and Ruth gain some peace after terrible times by wandering around the area early on summer mornings in *Martin Chuzzlewit*. Dickens himself was known to take rooms in the piazza when, for whatever reason, he could not get home of an evening: the offices of his fabulously successful weekly magazines *Household Words* (1850–59) and *All the Year Round* (1859–70) are just a few yards away on Wellington Street (there is a plaque) and he would sometimes work late. Often, he would end his famous night walks in Covent Garden, sometimes accompanied by Charles Frederick Field, a detective and later, private investigator on whom he is said to have based Inspector Bucket in *Bleak House*. In 1851 Dickens wrote an article *On Duty with Inspector Field* for *Household Words* which detailed their wanderings among the poorest underclass of the city at night. It is vintage Dickens as it begins:

> How goes the night? Saint Giles's clock is striking nine. The weather is dull and wet, and the long lines of street lamps are blurred, as if we saw them through tears. A damp wind blows and rakes the pieman's fire out, when he opens the door of his little furnace, carrying away an eddy of sparks ....

He meets up with Inspector Field and, proceeding to St Giles, New Oxford Street and surroundings, they come across an old outhouse, open the door:

> ...and let us look! Ten, twenty, thirty – who can count them! Men, women, children, for the most part naked, heaped upon the floor like maggots in a cheese!

All the while Mr Field holds sway and is respected, even though 'he has collared half the people here, and motioned their brothers, sisters, fathers, mothers, male and female friends, inexorably to New South Wales.'

Field was, according to Dickens, 'a portly presence with a large, moist knowing eye', and, like Holmes a few years later, fond of drama, disguises, and unconventional behaviour, sometimes, his police colleagues complained, to the point of embarrassment. He became famous, helped in no small part by his association with the greatest novelist of the age, and was beloved by the press before his death in 1874 – perhaps the first English detective, official or otherwise, real or fictional, to beguile the general public.

From this spot you can wander in all directions and see the great theatres of London and check out what is playing. This walk, though, carries on down Wellington Street in the general direction of the river. At the bottom of the road to your right you will see the impressive portico and six large columns of the Lyceum Theatre and it is 'by the third pillar from the left ... tonight at seven o'clock' that Miss Mary Morstan is requested to meet a mysterious person in *The Sign of Four*. She is told she can bring two friends, so Holmes and Watson accompany her and they are soon all transported by clattering cab to Thaddeus Sholto's unusual house.

This walk ends here; the Strand is off to your right, Aldwych, Fleet Street and St Paul's to your left and Waterloo Bridge straight ahead.

WALK 5

London: At the centre of Government – a walk in Westminster and Victoria

At A Glance – the following stories, plays and novels are highlighted in this walk:

The Crooked Man. The Hound of the Baskervilles. The Five Orange Pips. The Adventure of Charles Augustus Milverton. The Adventure of the Blue Carbuncle. The Adventure of the Abbey Grange. The Adventure of the Cardboard Box. A Study in Scarlet. The Adventure of the Engineer's Thumb. The Disappearance of Lady Frances Carfax. The Sign of Four. The Naval Treaty. The Musgrave Ritual. The Adventure of the Second Stain. The Lost World. Micah Clarke. Silver Blaze. The Final Problem. The Adventure of Wisteria Lodge. The Adventure of the Bruce-Partington Plans. A Case of Identity. The Adventure of the Noble Bachelor. The Adventure of Black Peter. The Adventure of the Empty House. The Adventure of the Priory School. The Greek Interpreter. The 'Gloria Scott'

Distance: About 6 kilometres/3.7 miles

Time to allow: A complete day for the walking. This is the longest route in the book. If you add on the time to spend exploring the sites on the way – Palace of Westminster, Westminster Abbey, Buckingham Palace and others – it can take several very enjoyable days. One idea is to walk the route first and then return on subsequent days to explore sites that particularly appeal.

Walking conditions: It can be breezy over Hungerford Bridge and Golden Jubilee Foot Bridges; there are steps up and down but also a lift. Thereafter, in the main, flat or very gently sloping but with very heavy traffic in parts, e.g., Parliament Square, around Victoria Station and Trafalgar Square. There are some spectacular views, for example, from Hungerford Bridge and in Parliament Square, so take a camera!

64   On the Trail of Sherlock Holmes

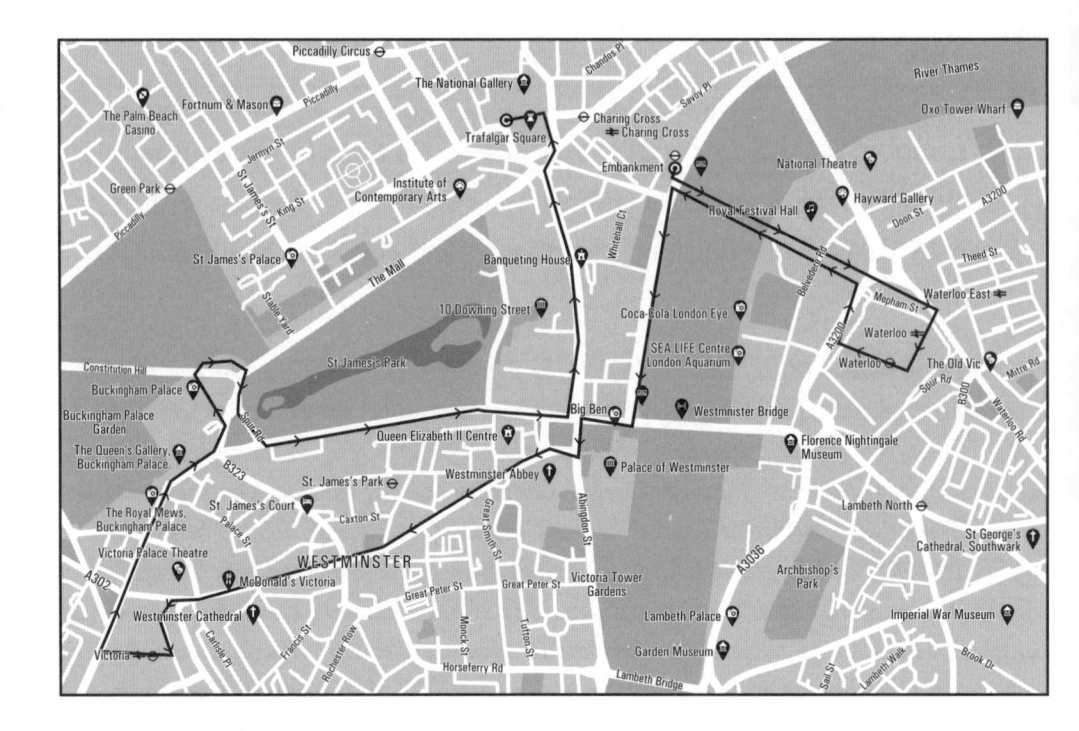

Route
- Embankment tube station
- Hungerford Bridge
- Waterloo station
- Victoria Embankment
- Westminster Bridge
- Parliament Square
- Victoria Street
- Buckingham Palace
- Birdcage Walk
- Whitehall

This is the second walk to begin at Embankment tube – District (green), Circle (yellow), Bakerloo (brown) and Northern (black) lines. This time, though, we are heading across the water to Waterloo and the reason for starting here is to experience the vistas from both sides of the Golden Jubilee Foot Bridges – the east side, to Waterloo and, after a consideration of the Waterloo station in the stories, the west side on the way back. The views of London both down- and up-river are fabulous and make for one of the best free spectacles in the city.

The foot bridges were designed by Lifschutz Davidson Sandilands and won a specialist award from the Royal Fine Art Commission in 2003 in the 'Building of the Year' Awards. In 2014 a Garden Bridge was briefly proposed for the river; although the idea has now been dropped, an assessment of the use of the Golden Jubilee Foot Bridges at the time estimated them to be the busiest in London with a footfall of 8.5 million each year.

Leave Embankment tube station by the entrance fronting the river. Take the east Golden Jubilee Foot Bridge and cross the Thames. Waterloo station itself is mentioned in eight of the stories, usually, as in *The Crooked Man*, when Holmes – 'I want to start by the 11.10 from Waterloo' – needs to take a train from there, or, in the same story, catches a bite to eat there on his way home. The 'new' Sir Henry Baskerville also arrives at the station in *The Hound of the Baskervilles*.

A more dramatic event occurs, however, towards the end of *The Five Orange Pips*, and one which leaves Holmes more depressed and shaken than Watson had ever seen his friend, spurring him on to finally tie up the loose ends in the case. He and Watson are both at breakfast when they see a headline in the morning paper: 'Tragedy near Waterloo Bridge'. The report goes on to say that young John Openshaw, who had come to Holmes for help, has been accidentally killed when he slipped on one of the small landing places for river steamers when rushing for the last train from Waterloo. Of course, it is no accident and Holmes announces that he is going out. Watson asks if he is going to the police. 'No, I shall be my own police,' replies Holmes.

The tales always gain an extra layer of excitement when Holmes takes the law into his own hands, maybe as in *The Five Orange Pips* because he knows that only he has the abilities to identify the culprits, or occasionally, as in *The Adventure of Charles Augustus Milverton*, in a blatantly criminal act of breaking and entering, or where he appoints himself both judge and jury as at the end of *The Adventure of the Blue Carbuncle* when he lets the wretched, terrified miscreant go, uttering the immortal words: 'I am not retained by the police to supply their deficiencies'. At the end of *The Adventure of the Abbey Grange* it is Watson who acts as the jury and is asked by Holmes for a verdict on Crocker, who had killed Sir Eustace but has no regrets whatsoever given the circumstances. Watson says 'Not guilty' and Holmes lets Crocker go free. The moral aspects of the adventures are clearly affected by Holmes and Watson operating outside the law and fans have strong opinions on this topic as can be seen in the conversations on Sherlock Holmes Facebook pages and online forums.

It is also near Waterloo that John Clayton, the cabbie Holmes was keen to track down – in *The Hound of the Baskervilles* – kept his horse and cart (he gives the fictional address of 3 Turpey Street, Southwark and he kept his cab in Shipley's Yard).

London Waterloo station was first opened in 1848 – it was never designed to be a terminus but a through station on the way into the city. Six years later, by special Act of Parliament in response to panic caused by the closure of London graveyards, a route serving Brookwood Cemetery was opened by The London Necropolis and National Mausoleum Company with its own platform, station and ticketing arrangements. The station became a byword for confusion by the end of the nineteenth century as fewer numbers were allocated for platforms than were necessary and some numbers were used twice. Jerome K. Jerome had fun with this as his travellers in the 1899 novel *Three Men in a Boat* struggle to find their train to Kingston upon Thames with seemingly every official on the station giving them conflicting advice.

The main station has a huge clock in the middle of the concourse, constructed in the 1920s, which you cannot miss and which is known as the lovers' clock – many romantic meetings, both real and on film, have taken place underneath.

From 1994 to 2007 the station served as the London end of Eurostar, but in 1998 the BBC reported that some travellers from France were upset by arriving at a station named after Napoleon's final defeat by the British and Prussians; some French councillors requested, to no avail, a change of name from 'Waterloo'. Since 2007, Eurostar travellers have needed to go to St Pancras, the meaning of which is not universally agreed but at least has not to date caused controversy – it may derive from St Pancratius, a Roman citizen who was executed at the age of 14 for converting to Christianity.

Waterloo station concourse is vast with a fair array of retail shops, including a bookshop. There are plenty of places to eat and drink, and toilets. When you are ready to leave, follow the signs to the Golden Jubilee Foot Bridges. The west footbridge travels from the south to the north bank. When on land, walk along the Victoria Embankment with the river on your left.

The Great Stink

In 1858, as MPs shuddered behind curtains soaked in chloride of lime to minimise the stench of human excrement from the Thames, and Disraeli said that the Thames had become 'a Stygian pool reeking with ineffable and unbearable horror', it was at last agreed that something must be done. The problem derived from centuries of pumping human, and every other form, of waste into the River Thames; it was seen as an Imperial issue as well – the British Empire was stinking and rotting from its core.

The solution as envisaged by Joseph Bazelgette, a monument to whom you will pass as you walk on the river's edge, involved the most ambitious urban engineering project ever undertaken – embanking the Thames to create the Victoria, Albert and Chelsea embankments and the digging of a vast underground sewage system still in use today. Bazalgette is usually seen as one of the great, almost unsung, heroes of London, in large part because his influence on people's health was profound yet his magnificent 'cathedral of sewage' is not visible above ground. It is possible, however, to visit the intricate and colourful Crossness Victorian pumping station. Trips can be made by those who are firm of foot along the sewers themselves.[34]

The Victoria Embankment along which you are walking was begun in 1865 and finished five years later. It involved narrowing the river by building out into it. Whitehall Gardens, on the other side of the roadway, was also built at this time. In 1878 this stretch became the first street in Britain to be permanently lit with electricity.

On your right you will see, not far from Big Ben, the Norman Shaw Buildings, unmistakeable due to their 'stripes' of red brick and white Portland stone. This was the New Scotland Yard known to Sherlock Holmes and used between 1890 and 1967, after which the building became government offices. During construction in 1888 the torso of a woman was discovered by workers – the rest of her was never found. At first seen as possibly a medical prank, the ghastly find was later linked to Jack the Ripper, but again, this theory was dismissed by the police. It became known as The Whitehall Mystery and the case has never been solved – the press at the time, and subsequently, not failing to note the irony of the new London police HQ being built on the scene of an unsolved murder.

Holmes worked with twenty-three Inspectors from New Scotland Yard, the most famous of whom were Lestrade, Tobias Gregson and Stanley Hopkins.[35] Lestrade's initial is stated to be 'G' in *The Adventure of the Cardboard Box* and the family name may derive from a friend of Conan Doyle at Edinburgh University, Joseph Lestrade. In the worldwide hit BBC series *Sherlock* (2010–17) written by Mark Gatiss, Steven Moffat and Stephen Thompson, a running joke is that Sherlock Holmes, as played by Benedict Cumberbatch, can never remember Lestrade's first name. He is stated in the canon to be 'a little sallow rat-faced, dark-eyed fellow' (*A Study in Scarlet*), who succeeds largely because of his tenacity rather than his crime-solving skills. He appears thirteen times in the canon and Holmes seems quite fond of him, allowing him to unduly take the credit for some cases. Lestrade and Tobias Gregson are 'the best of a bad lot'.

More often than not, the detectives join Holmes in Baker Street or at the scene of the crime. As an exception to the rule in *The Adventure of the Engineer's Thumb*, Holmes says 'we shall go down to Scotland Yard at once', where he, Watson and Victor Hatherley pick up Inspector Bradstreet before taking the train to Eyford. Again, in *The Disappearance of Lady Frances Carfax*, Holmes tells Watson that in the evening he will walk down to Scotland Yard and have a word with 'friend Lestrade'. On screen, however, Scotland Yard tends to play a bigger role; in some of the many TV series, such as the excellent but rarely seen 1979 series *Sherlock Holmes and Doctor Watson*, created by Sheldon Reynolds and starring Geoffrey Whitehead as Holmes, Donald Pickering as Watson and Patrick Newell as Lestrade, for example, key scenes take place in Lestrade's office in Scotland Yard.[36]

After the case of the Yorkshire Ripper in 1985, the police developed the Home Office Large Major Enquiry System (HOLMES), an administrative support system for senior officers dealing with major crime in UK police forces. It was named in honour of Sherlock Holmes. An updated version, HOLMES2, is now used by all British forces.

As you approach Westminster Bridge, cast your eyes to the other side of the river to see Westminster Stairs, adjoining the bridge and leading down to the water. In *The Sign of Four*, as the chase up the Thames is on, Holmes says to Athelney Jones: 'Well then, in the first place I shall want a fast police boat – a steam launch – to be at the Westminster Stairs at seven o'clock.' Holmes then suggests that, when the expected treasure is in their hands, Watson should be the one to take it round to its rightful owner who shall be the first to open the chest. Jones thinks the whole thing highly irregular but accedes to the request, adding, '…I suppose we must wink at it'.

It is easy to see, in your mind's eye, a cab containing Holmes and Watson driving swiftly 'past the Houses of Parliament and over Westminster Bridge', as they discuss their next moves in *The Disappearance of Lady Frances Carfax*. The story is one of the more unsettling in the canon with aspects of a horror story (the prospect of being buried alive while chloroformed). It has been adapted and amended several times – for instance in the Granada production (1984–94) starring Jeremy Brett, the adventure takes place in the Lake District and it is also heavily altered in the CBS series *Elementary* (2012–19) starring Jonny Lee Miller and Lucy Liu where it is called *The Ballad of Lady Frances*.

Westminster Bridge and the Arts

Westminster Bridge features in many English poems, novels and films. Jane Austen, in *Emma* (1815) mentions a visit to Astley's Theatre which was situated just over the far side of the bridge (from where you are standing now) and Wilkie Collins recalled a visit to the same theatre with enormous affection; Pip mentions the bridge in *Great Expectations* and Charles Dickens sets scenes here in both *David Copperfield* and *Barnaby Rudge*; Jim, played by Cillian Murphy, walks across the eerily deserted bridge in the film *28 Days Later* (directed by Danny Boyle, 2002) and James Bond finds himself confronting his nemesis on the bridge after Blofeld's helicopter crashes on it in *Spectre* (Eon Productions 2015). The most famous poem associated with the bridge, in fact, some claim the most famous poem about London in the English Language, is *Composed upon Westminster Bridge, September 3, 1802* by William Wordsworth. He was travelling to Paris with his sister, Dorothy, when his carriage stopped on the bridge.

> Earth has not anything to show more fair:
> Dull would he be of soul who could pass by
> A sight so touching in its majesty:
> This City now doth, like a garment, wear
> The beauty of the morning; silent, bare,
> Ships, towers, domes, theatres, and temples lie
> Open unto the fields, and to the sky;
> All bright and glittering in the smokeless air.
> Never did sun more beautifully steep
> In his first splendour, valley, rock, or hill;
> Ne'er saw I, never felt, a calm so deep!
> The river glideth at his own sweet will:
> Dear God! the very houses seem asleep;
> And all that mighty heart is lying still!

The poem has delighted, intrigued, and irritated people both at the time and since. As subject matter, it presents London as a romantic idealisation at the moment that Wordsworth sees it, yet this was the same putrid river that was to produce 'The Great Stink', just referred to, and it took many lives, providing for some a bare living, fraught with disease, as they scavenged in the mud for anything of value.[37]

Holmes around Big Ben and the Houses of Parliament

Big Ben looms straight ahead. Officially called Elizabeth Tower it was designed by Augustus Pugin and was his last commission before he succumbed to madness. On finally submitting the plans he is reported to have said about his creation '...it is beautiful'. Completed in 1859, it has 334 steps up to the belfry (a lift is being installed at the time of writing). It has developed a tilt – about 20 inches at the top – but it is estimated that this should not be a critical problem for a few thousand years. In *The Naval Treaty* it is presumably Big Ben that young Phelps hears at his office in Charles Street – we are not told for sure but there are no other striking clocks around here – when he determines it is a quarter to ten, a fact that Holmes says is of enormous importance in ascertaining how the documents which have been stolen, vanished.

Turn right into Parliament Square for a more comprehensive view of the Palace of Westminster, usually known as the Houses of Parliament. Reginald Musgrave becomes an MP following his father's death in *The Musgrave Ritual*. The fictitious 16 Godolphin Street, 'one of the old-fashioned and secluded rows of eighteenth century houses which lie between the river and the Abbey, almost in the shadow of the Great Tower of the Houses of Parliament', is where Mr Eduardo Lucas was stabbed through the heart with a curved Indian dagger in *The Adventure of the Second Stain*. Great Peter Street, by contrast, does exist and it was to Holmes' 'dirty little lieutenant Wiggins' that a wire was dispatched from the Post Office here in *The Sign of Four*. Holmes explains to Watson that the 'Baker Street division of the detective police force' might be invaluable for the task in hand – to find the whereabouts of the steam launch *Aurora* – as they can 'go everywhere, see everything, overhear everyone'.

Conan Doyle twice stood for Parliament as outlined in Part 1. Why he did so was not clear to him. He certainly had no great desire to sit in Parliament and had also been offered easier seats than those he fought. There was a certain romanticism to fighting Central Edinburgh, which might have been a fine exploit if he were one of his more dashing literary characters, but he came to the conclusion that he did it primarily to have a go, to put himself in the way of life, to give himself an opportunity to win if fate so decreed. He also thought that the hustings were an excellent training ground for standing tall when speaking despite hecklers and all sorts of distractions and that this was to stand him in good stead when he came to promote the ultimate point of his life – his spiritual work.

Westminster Abbey is here. Many poets and writers are commemorated in Poets' Corner.[38] This does not include Sir Arthur Conan Doyle, who is buried in Minstead in the New Forest, having first been laid to rest in the rose garden of his home, Windlesham. He was not a Christian, regarding himself as a Spiritualist. There have been campaigns to have him given at least a plaque in the abbey but this has not happened yet. All his life he knew the abbey very well and there are some records of his activities and visits here – for example, he came at the age of 15 on a visit from his Jesuit Stonyhurst School; he attended the funeral of Sir Henry Irving at the abbey in October 1905; in *The Lost World*, published in 1912, he writes that the pugnacious Professor Challenger, who liked to assault curious journalists, believed 'he was destined for Westminster Abbey'; and in

1925, he helped set up the ill-fated Psychic bookshop in nearby Victoria Street. Yet, curiously, Sherlock Holmes does not have adventures here.

This walk continues down Victoria Street. At the beginning of *The Adventure of the Engineer's Thumb,* Watson explains that there have been two cases which he has introduced to Sherlock Holmes: that of Colonel Warburton's madness (the details of which presumably still lie in the tin trunk entrusted to Cox and Co. in Charing Cross) and this one. A young man, Mr Victor Hatherley, has been brought round by a member of railway staff from nearby Paddington station. His card shows that his address is 16A, Victoria Street (3rd floor). He has a horrific injury caused by something like a meat cleaver. Watson says:

'An accident, I presume?'
'By no means.'
'What! A murderous attack?'
'Very murderous indeed.'
'You horrify me.'

At Watson's suggestion they rush around to Sherlock Holmes, and Conan Doyle must surely have chuckled to himself as he has the young man tell of the loneliness of starting up a business – it sounds very similar to Conan Doyle's customer-less days in Upper Wimpole Street, referred to in Walk 1. The young man has had his offices for two years, during which he has had three consultations and gross takings which total just £27 10s.

At the end of this wide street, opened in 1851 and named after Queen Victoria, lies Victoria Station. In the summer of 1889 Conan Doyle arrived here and took a cab to the Langham Hotel where he first met Oscar Wilde and he was smitten immediately. They were both the guests of Joseph Stoddart, managing editor of *Lippincott's Monthly,* a Philadelphia magazine. He was planning an English edition. Doyle wrote later of this 'golden evening' during which Wilde praised Doyle's just-published novel, *Micah Clarke.* Conan Doyle wrote of the meeting with Wilde that his conversation left an indelible impression, that he has delicacy and tact, and that he 'towered above us all'.

The two men left with commissions – Doyle for *The Sign of Four* and Wilde for *The Picture of Dorian Gray,* both of which appeared in the new magazine. Conan Doyle wrote in his diary on 30 August 1889, of which a copy exists, that he has been offered '£100 for 45,000 words for Lippincott's'. It has been suggested that Wilde advocated a darker side to Holmes as the next adventure, *The Sign of Four*, starts with Holmes' cocaine habit; also, that Thaddeus Sholto in the tale is, in fact, Wilde. Both of these things are incapable of proof unless some further evidence comes to light. In future years Doyle saw Wilde once more and thought he had become mad. He said of his fall from grace that what ruined him was in essence a pathological, not a criminal, issue and that a hospital rather than a police cell was where he should have been sent.

Following Wilde's death, Doyle was completely convinced that he had contacted Wilde in seances, in particular because of some typical witty opinions, one of which was to the effect that death is the most boring thing there is apart from being married or having dinner with a schoolmaster.

Conan Doyle regarded that, through the meeting with Stoddart and Wilde, he 'touched the edge of literary society'. There was only one previous time that he considered this had been accomplished. This was at a dinner at the Ship at Greenwich to which he was invited on account of his contributions to *Cornhill* magazine. Here he met a man he had long esteemed, the author James Payn (1830–98). He was waiting for a statement of significance from the great man but his first words were that the window was cracked and he wondered how this had occurred. He subsequently found that there was no wittier or delightful companion in the world. Here he also met F. Anstey, a pseudonym for Thomas Anstey Guthrie (1856–1934) who was having great success with his comic novel *Vice Versa*, which detailed how a father and son had swapped bodies after the son discovered a magic stone; the father goes to the boy's school and the boy runs his father's business before they swap back again, both much chastened by their experiences. The book has been filmed at least five times. Following this dinner Conan Doyle came home 'floating on air'.

Victoria Station is used a few times in the stories but much less than Waterloo – one such is when Holmes and Watson return by rail from *Silver Blaze*: 'This is Clapham Junction,' says Holmes. 'If I am not mistaken, we shall be in Victoria in less than ten minutes.' A more intricate plan to catch a train here is made by Watson in *The Final Problem* and discussed in Walk 2.

From Victoria Station take Grosvenor Gardens heading in the direction of Buckingham Palace. Here, in *The Adventure of Wisteria Lodge*, at the Spanish Embassy (1 Grosvenor Square), Mr Scott Eccles enquires about Garcia only to find that no one at the embassy knows him.

Buckingham Palace is an extended and modified version of Buckingham House, built for the Duke of Buckingham in 1703. It is the London residence of the monarch of the United Kingdom and has 775 rooms and the largest private garden in London.

Sherlock Holmes and Royalty

Holmes was very much at home with royalty and unswervingly patriotic, although nowhere in the canon does he actually meet Queen Victoria. This may have something to do with the fact Conan Doyle remarked that he himself had little acquaintance with kings and queens – although we know that this is not totally true: there is on record a dinner at which he sat at the same table as Edward VII and it is said that the king, who was also a Sherlock Holmes fan, recommended him for his knighthood – because he was so busy and preoccupied. A royal visit may be accurately deduced, however, at the end of *The Adventure of the Bruce-Partington Plans*, where he spends a day in Windsor and returns with a remarkably fine emerald tie-pin. Watson asks where it came from and Holmes replies that it was a gift from a 'certain gracious lady in whose interests he had once been fortunate enough to carry out a small commission'. His most notable expression of patriotism, amusingly to Watson's (and Mrs Hudson's) fierce disapproval was when, at the start of *The Musgrave Ritual*, he, 'in one of his queer humours', sits in an armchair 'with his hair-trigger and a hundred boxer cartridges', and adorns the opposite wall with a 'V.R.' (Victoria Regina) in bullet-pocks.

He is also well-acquainted with various other royals. At the start of *A Case of Identity*, Watson remarks on the splendour of a snuffbox of old gold, with a great amethyst in the centre of the lid and Holmes tells him that this is a gift from the King of Bohemia for his help with the Irene Adler Papers. In a very funny exchange, as *The Adventure of the Noble Bachelor* gets under way, Lord St Simon is rash enough to imply that, should Holmes take his case, he will be mixing in a higher class of society than he is used to.

'No. I am descending.'
'I beg pardon.'
'My last client was a sort of a king.'
'Oh. I really had no idea. And which king?'
'The King of Scandinavia.'

Percy Phelps is talking to Watson in *The Naval Treaty*, seeking reassurance as to Holmes' credentials in dealing with crucial matters of state. 'To my certain knowledge,' Watson tells him, 'he has acted on behalf of three of the reigning houses of Europe in very vital matters.' It is hardly a surprise to learn, also, that when he was 'dead' for three years he amused himself by visiting Lhassa and 'spending some days with the head lama'. Again, we learn, in *The Adventure of Black Peter*, that Holmes investigated the sudden death of Cardinal Tosca 'at the express desire of His Holiness the Pope'.

Several of the most memorable cases involve the aristocracy. Charles Augustus Milverton's unscrupulous and immoral behaviour centres around the marriage of Lady Eva Blackwell. The murdered young Ronald Adair in *The Adventure of the Empty House*, was the second son of the Earl of Maynooth, 'governor of one of the Australian colonies'. Generally, the nobility is seen as upright but, in *The Adventure of the Priory School*, Holmes unmasks the duplicity of the illustrious Duke of Holdernesse, from whom he requests a cheque for six thousand pounds when the case is solved:

'The Duke fell back in his chair.
'And whom do you accuse?'
Sherlock Holmes's answer was an astounding one. He stepped swiftly forward and touched the Duke upon the shoulder.
'I accuse *you*,' he said. 'And now, your Grace, I'll trouble you for that cheque.'

As we learn that Mycroft, Sherlock's brother, has a unique position where on occasion he *is* the British government, it is natural that the Prime Minister himself is directed to Holmes in *The Adventure of the Second Stain*. On a Tuesday morning in autumn a visitor to Baker Street, 'austere, high-nosed, eagle-eyed and dominant, was none other than the illustrious Lord Bellinger, twice Premier of Britain'. Billy, the young page, has some sagacious words about these political grandees who come to see Holmes, as we find out at the beginning of *The Adventure of the Mazarin Stone*. He comically says that he gets along just fine with the Prime Minister and has nothing against the Home Secretary but cannot stand Lord Cantlemere.

In real life, Conan Doyle knew royalty and top brass and their meetings are outlined in various parts of this study. One occasion was in in April 1917 when he was invited to breakfast by Lloyd George, Prime Minister of the United Kingdom 1916–22. Conan Doyle found him relaxed and smiling, clad in a grey suit and, as there were no servants present, the Prime Minister poured out the tea while Conan Doyle brought bacon and eggs for both from a side table. There is scant record of the conversation but it is safe to say it was probably at least partially about soldiering and armaments as Conan Doyle had a habit, found irksome by some in authority, of making many suggestions and had personally written to Lloyd George on these topics.

Following the Boer War Conan Doyle had become convinced that the primary weapon of war was the rifle, or machine gun, which was a 'modified rifle'. He founded the 'Undershaw Club' which was inspected by Lord Roberts and became the model for many more rifle clubs throughout the land. He wrote to *The Times* suggesting that a law be passed compelling all parish councils to establish a rifle club. In answer to the criticism that such activities were not suitable for the Christian Sabbath, he said that training to help one's country was, for young men, preferable to standing around on road corners, and in a subsequent letter pointed out that shooting, motoring, golf, boating and cycling were already universal on Sundays.[39]

Conan Doyle was a great traveller and recounts how he received a message from the Sultan, when visiting Constantinople between the wars, saying that he had read the author's books and would gladly have seen him had it not been Ramadan. He did, however, award him the Order of the Medjedie (a military and civilian Order instituted in 1851 and often awarded to non-Turkish nationals) and, pleasing Conan Doyle much more, granted his wife the Order of Chevekat (the Order of Compassion).

As regards the British Empire, both Holmes and Conan Doyle were children of their time. When visiting Canada, Conan Doyle saw everywhere a consciousness of the Empire's glory and was convinced that it had a magnificent future. When this sentiment was added to the material advantages of the arrangement, he saw no reason for Canada to seek independence.

Leave the Buckingham Palace locale by Birdcage Walk. The unusual name derives from the fact that the Royal Aviary and Menagerie were here in the reign of James I. Keep St James' Park on your left – this was used in the filming of the BBC series *Sherlock* and is probably the park that Sir Henry Baskerville walked around in *The Hound of the Baskervilles* when he had some time to kill and went out for some air; he does not specify the park but this would be the nearest to Northumberland Avenue. Turn left into Horse Guards Road and right at King Charles Street. Here you will find the Foreign Office, where Holmes would have briefed the government on his return after three years' absence. Percy Phelps ran to the side door on Charles Street, which he found unlocked, after he had discovered the missing documents in *The Naval Treaty*. There was no one outside, although great activity in Whitehall. Turn left into Whitehall. A short distance along on your left is Downing Street, home of the UK Prime Minister. It is also where Holmes and Watson were fortunate, after the theft of the naval treaty, in finding Lord Holdhurst, 'cabinet minister and future Prime Minister', still in his chambers as they needed to interview him. Mycroft also has his office here; in *The Greek Interpreter*, Conan Doyle writes, 'Mycroft lodges in Pall Mall, and he walks round the corner into Whitehall every morning and back every evening', and this is the only exercise he ever gets.

Facing Whitehall, nearing Trafalgar Square, you will see Admiralty House which, until 1964, was the official residence of the First Lords of the Admiralty. It is mentioned a few times in the stories, one of which is in *The 'Gloria Scott'*, as it was in this government department that the loss of the convict ship would have been registered. Ultimate responsibility for the Bruce-Partington plans rested here. It is also revealed in *The Adventure of the Priory School* that the Duke of Holdernesse had been Lord of the Admiralty in 1872. In real life, Conan Doyle had a ship named after him and it served more than honourably in the Great War.[40]

Whitehall leads into Trafalgar Square which is where this walk ends and the next begins.

78   On the Trail of Sherlock Holmes

WALK 6

London: Trafalgar Square, Pall Mall and Mayfair

At A Glance – the following stories, plays and novels are highlighted in this walk:

The Adventure of the Noble Bachelor. The Greek Interpreter. The Adventure of the Abbey Grange. The Adventure of the Three Gables. The Adventure of the Illustrious Client. The Adventure of Wisteria Lodge. The Adventure of Shoscombe Old Place. Raffles: The Amateur Cracksman (E.W. Hornung)

Distance: About 5.2 kilometres/3.3 miles

Time to allow: a morning, afternoon or evening for the walking itself – add on time to spend in the National Gallery, Royal Academy, Fortnum and Mason, National Portrait Gallery etc.

Walking conditions: Very busy in terms of pedestrians, buses and cars but basically flat. This is a beautiful part of London so take a camera!

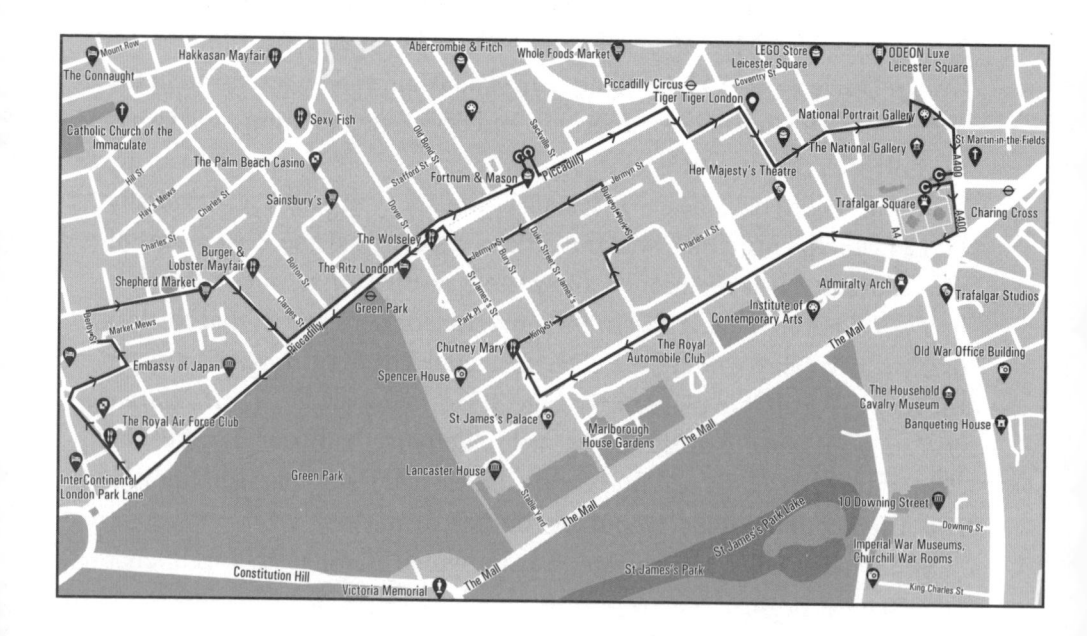

Walk 6: Mayfair   79

Route
- Trafalgar Square
- Pall Mall
- St James's Street
- King Street
- The London Library
- Old Park Lane
- Curzon Square
- Half Moon Street
- Piccadilly
- Charing Cross Road

If you have limited time and wish to take in some Sherlock Holmes sites, Trafalgar Square is a good base. From here you can walk up the Strand to Fleet Street and St Paul's (the second part of Walk 2) or take a trip to the river down Northumberland Avenue (the first part of Walk 2 but in reverse, so to speak). Then, there is this walk, travelling down Pall Mall and back along Piccadilly.

You can reach Trafalgar Square easily from several central tube stations: Charing Cross is nearest – Northern (black), Bakerloo (brown) and Jubilee (grey) lines – but it is a short walk from Leicester Square and Piccadilly stations also. All manner of bus routes have stops around the square.

The National Gallery, fronting Trafalgar Square, is a convenient spot for meeting up – either outside sitting along the low walls or inside where there are seats among the paintings, ideal for resting tired legs in magnificent surroundings, and a café with prices for a coffee or meal that are not ridiculous for central London. It is free to enter.

For this walk, take a 'roundabout' tour of the square as you stand looking out from the front of the National Gallery, and Pall Mall leads off on your right-hand side. In *The Adventure of the Noble Bachelor*, Holmes mockingly asks Lestrade, who has been busy supervising the dragging of the Serpentine for Lady St Simon: 'Have you dragged the basin of Trafalgar Square fountain?' He proceeds to explain: 'Because you have just a good a chance of finding this lady in the one as in the other.'

The square was built to celebrate the victory of Nelson over the combined French and Spanish fleets at the battle of Trafalgar in 1805. He has another column to his name, only slightly shorter than this one, in Great Yarmouth in Norfolk, where he used to land before visiting his wounded men in hospital (unusual at the time and one reason why he was followed so avidly by an adoring Norfolk press) before proceeding to London. The fountains were added in 1841, partly to reduce the heat resulting from the sun baking down onto such a large stretch of asphalt and also to reduce the amount of space for potentially riotous gatherings.

Turn into Pall Mall East which becomes Pall Mall. Several members' clubs were based in this part of Pall Mall – the Athenaeum, the Reform and the Carlton among them. Conan Doyle was a member of the first two and the Carlton is significant because the Diogenes Club is located 'a short distance away'. It is described in *The Greek Interpreter* as 'the queerest club in London', and 'Mycroft one of the queerest men.' He is always there, Watson is told, from quarter to five to twenty to eight. We meet Mycroft, his body 'absolutely corpulent', and he greets Watson by offering a 'broad, flat hand like the flipper of a seal'. He utters the famous lines: 'I hear of Sherlock everywhere since you became his chronicler.' Save in the Strangers Room no talking whatsoever is permitted; a scene of high comedy takes place in the BBC series *Sherlock* when John Watson (Martin Freeman) enters the club and horrifies members by speaking aloud to ask for Mycroft whereupon he is manhandled out by handlers wearing gloves and mufflers over their shoes.

Mycroft's lodgings are said in *The Greek Interpreter* to be opposite the club.

It is possible, although Conan Doyle does not say so, that the club was named after Diogenes the Cynic, and that it is a front for the British Secret Service, an idea explored by recent pastiches as well as in the BBC's *Sherlock*. Separately, in the CBS show *Elementary*, Mycroft owns a chain of restaurants called Diogenes.

The Royal Automobile Club was also headquartered here, at 69 Pall Mall. Conan Doyle was a member and a most enthusiastic driver which led to some of the most interesting storylines in the canon – this and his driving exploits in Norfolk are discussed in Chapter 8.

In *The Adventure of the Abbey Grange*, Holmes investigates, on behalf of 'friend Hopkins', a Scotland Yard inspector for whom he saw a bright future, the operations of the Adelaide-Southampton shipping line which stands 'at the end of Pall Mall if I remember right'.

Turn right into St James's Street. This is where Conan Doyle introduces a 'strange, languid creature' who spends his waking hours in the bow window of a St James's club where he becomes the custodian, and seller to the gutter press of the day, of all the gossip in the metropolis. His name is Langdale Pike and it is to him that Holmes turns for essential information in *The Adventure of the Three Gables*.

Turning right again into King Street will bring you to St James's Square and the London Library. It is to this library that Watson comes – not the British Library – when Holmes asks him to spend the next twenty-four hours in an intensive study of Chinese pottery in *The Adventure of the Illustrious Client*. He leaves, having consulted his friend Lomax, the sub-librarian, with a 'goodly volume' under his arm, his studies leading to not entirely anticipated results at the beautiful house of Baron Gruner.

The London Library came into being as a result of Thomas Carlyle declaring on 24 June 1840 that London needed a new central library. It now has over a million books and periodicals and 6,500 members who in the past have included, Kipling, Thackeray, Tennyson, Woolf, E.M. Forster, Agatha Christie, Lawrence Olivier, Sigrid Sassoon, Elgar, Winston Churchill, Kazuo Ishiguro and Henry Irving. Over time, five Poets Laureate and ten Nobel Prize winners have been members. Membership is available.[41]

The walk proceeds back to St James's Street and then left along Piccadilly. Holmes and Watson cross this famous street on their way to the Diogenes Club. Keeping Green Park to your left follow this affluent concourse until you see Old Park Lane on your right. This leads onto Park Lane and then Curzon Square. This is where the police lose Murillo and Lopez in *The Adventure of Wisteria Lodge*. At the top of the square, take Curzon Street and follow it along. This is the location, given in *The Adventure of Shoscombe Old Place*, of Sam Brewer, the well-known Curzon Street money lender who was whipped, Holmes says, on Newmarket Heath. Carry on and take Half Moon Street on your right and follow it down to Piccadilly. Watson gave the address of 369 Half Moon Street and his name as Dr Hill Barton to Baron Gruner when assuming the guise of an expert in Chinese pottery as detailed above. With Green Park ahead of you across the road, turn left along Piccadilly.

This street became famous for the manufacture of piccadills – large fancy collars often of lace that became fashionable in the 1600s – and hence was known as 'Piccadilly'. It is said to have inspired Oscar Wilde's *The Importance of Being Earnest*. Here are some famous establishments – such as the Ritz Hotel, Burlington Arcade, Fortnum and Mason, Hatchards bookshop, and The Royal Academy of Arts.

Raffles

> 'Money lost – little lost. Honour lost – much lost. Pluck lost – all lost.'
>
> E. W. Hornung, *Raffles, The Amateur Cracksman*

Just before Sackville Street, on the same side, lies the Albany or simply Albany, an apartment block converted for the well-to-do young men about town in 1802. It was here that Conan Doyle's brother-in-law, E.W. Hornung, set *Raffles: The Amateur Cracksman*. He first discussed the idea with Conan Doyle, who was encouraging. The twenty-six stories and one novel – about half of Conan Doyle's total 'Holmes' output – were a great contemporary success and have stood the test of time more than Hornung's other writing.

With regard to Willie Hornung's sharpness and humour, Conan Doyle, wrote that he 'was a Dr Johnson without the learning' (Conan Doyle was to give a talk on Dr Johnson in the Cheddar Cheese pub in 1926; more details in Walk 2), and that he had a quickness of brain which produced many memorable quotes, one of which, well known to Sherlockians, is about Conan Doyle's creation: 'Though he might be more humble, there is no police like Holmes.'

Raffles first appeared in an 1898 story *The Ides of March* and for the last time in the 1909 novel *Mr Justice Raffles*. Raffles is a 'gentleman thief', living at the Albany who also plays cricket as an 'amateur' for England and as he is very good at it, especially spin bowling and dashing off the odd hundred, gains a fame that he uses to infiltrate the moneyed classes, whom he robs although always according to a code of honour: he will not rob his host and he would rather not kill (although he does once). He is joined by his 'Watson' in the form of Bunny Manders, whom he saves from suicide and bankruptcy. Bunny has idolised Raffles since they were at public school together where Bunny was Raffles' fag (a kind of personal servant). Now 28 and 24 as opposed to 18 and 14, they have a very strong and intimate relationship and it has been suggested that Raffles is based on a friend of Hornung's, the talented cricketer George Ives, who also lived at the Albany and was privately homosexual.[42]

> 'Again, I see him, leaning back in one of the luxurious chairs with which his room was furnished. I see his indolent, athletic figure; his pale, sharp, clean-shaven features; his curly black hair; his strong, unscrupulous mouth. And again, I feel the clear beam of his wonderful eye, cold and luminous as a star, shining.'
>
> E.W. Hornung, *The Complete Raffles Collection*

In his influential 1944 essay *Raffles and Miss Blandish*, George Orwell addresses Hornung's writing and the appeal of Raffles as a character. He considered Hornung a very able writer 'on his level' and the reason Raffles continued to have appeal was that he was a *gentleman*.

These two *gentlemen* – for Bunny is cut from the same cloth – begin a series of very exciting adventures together that happen to be illegal, often breaking into safes and stealing the fabulous jewels within. *The Strand Magazine* regarded Raffles as the second most popular fictional character of the era, behind their main attraction, Sherlock Holmes. In *The Gift of the Emperor* their luck runs out with Raffles presumed dead and Bunny serving time in prison. Raffles is not dead, however, and they reunite, very much changed – older now, world-weary and acting as outlaws. Volunteering for the Boer War, Raffles is killed and Bunny returns to England to write his memoirs. Many applauded such a sticky and sad finale as an example that criminality will not win through.

Conan Doyle wrote that Raffles was 'a kind of inversion of Sherlock Holmes' and that Bunny was his Watson. He regarded the tales as very fine examples of short story writing but they had one very serious flaw – they were dangerous in their suggestion that the criminal could be a hero.

> 'I was afraid I wrote neither well enough nor ill enough for success.'
>
> E.W. Hornung

Raffles and Holmes have been linked in literature on innumerable occasions since they both first appeared. Almost immediately on Raffles' release into the literary world, John Kendrick Bangs, a prolific and popular American author, published *R. Holmes and Co*, which featured Raffles Holmes (Sherlock Holmes' son and Raffles' grandson). He also wrote *Mrs Raffles*, which sees Bunny in America. The two duos have also, in novels, been pitted against each other and sent into space, as well as making cameo appearances, or at least have been mentioned, in all manner of stories including *Dracula* and *Dr Who*. At the present time there is a thriving revival of pastiche literature featuring Raffles and Bunny.

Six films were made before 1939, and the 1977 series for TV with Christopher Strauli as Bunny and Anthony Valentine as Raffles was successful, but despite their undeniable hold on the public imagination, the pair are yet to break free from the overwhelmingly greater shadow of Holmes and Watson.

Leaving the Albany, turn left and follow Piccadilly to Piccadilly Circus, where the second hostage scene was filmed for BBC's *Sherlock* (2010). Other sites in this locale are discussed in Walk 3.

From here, the walk proceeds to Charing Cross Road. There are many ways to get there as this is one of the most interesting parts of the city with a criss-cross of roads running south of Leicester Square, but in this walk we drop down Regent Street, turn left along Jermyn Street, right into the Haymarket and left into Orange Street which leads to Charing Cross Road and the National Portrait Gallery. This is a good final stop on the walk as in room 31, at the time of writing, is a fine portrait of Sir Arthur Conan Doyle; it is by Henry L. Gates, dated 1927 and was given by Conan Doyle's daughter, Dame Jean Bromet. The National Gallery, where this walk began, is just around the corner.

WALK 7

London: A walk around the City and East End

At A Glance – the following stories, plays and novels are highlighted in this walk:

The Red-headed League. The Adventure of the Sussex Vampire. The Stockbroker's Clerk. The Man with the Twisted Lip. The Adventure of the Blanched Soldier. A Case of Identity. The Adventure of the Bruce-Partington Plans. The Adventure of the Mazarin Stone. The Five Orange Pips. The Sign of Four

Distance: About 5.1 kilometres/3.2 miles. At Bank the walk stops for a break and details several possible short 'excursions' out and back again – in total, these probably add about 2 kilometres/1.2 miles.

Time to allow: A complete day as it is almost inevitable that you will wander off course here and there or find an alley or street that merits an extra look in this fascinating part of London. It is also very easy to become temporarily lost with all the criss-crossing lanes and passageways around these parts. In terms of general interest – as opposed to places of interest specifically to Holmes' fans – the walk passes close by the Museum of London, the Bank of England Museum and ends at the Tower of London, all of which merit a stay of at least an hour or two.

Walking conditions: A mix of business and more touristy areas, so quite busy with many places to eat and drink along the route. No steep slopes. Take a camera to capture especially scenic parts of the walk such as Smithfield Market, Monument or the Tower of London.

86   On the Trail of Sherlock Holmes

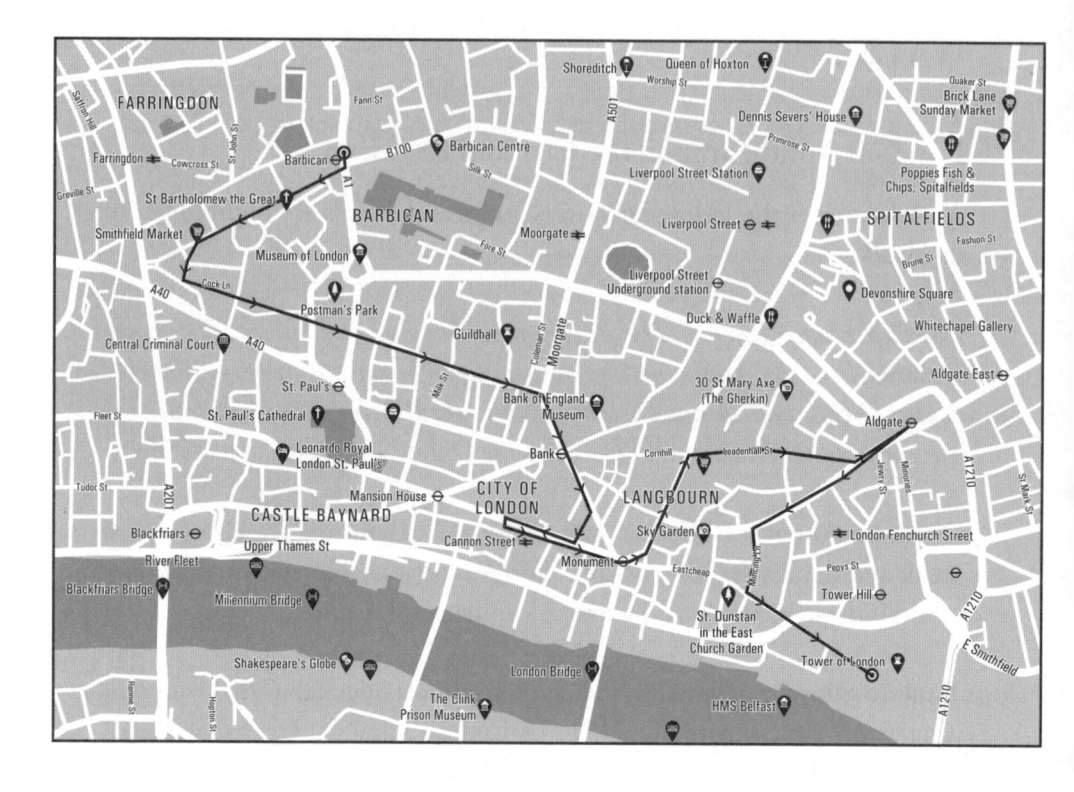

Route
- Barbican tube station
- Charterhouse Street
- Smithfield Market
- Bank
- Cannon Street station
- Monument
- Cornhill
- Leadenhall Street
- Aldgate High Street
- Fenchurch Street
- Mincing Lane
- Tower Hill
- Tower of London

The walk begins at Barbican tube station, served by the Circle, Hammersmith and City and Metropolitan lines – Aldersgate until 1924. It is to this station that Holmes and Watson come during *The Red-headed*

League to find Jabez Wilson's small pawnbroker's shop which is 'a short walk away' in Saxe-Coburg Square, 'a poky, little, shabby-genteel place'. Holmes is in super-mysterious mood as he thumps the ground around the shop with his stick before asking the man who answers the door how to get to the Strand; he confides afterwards to Watson that they have just encountered the fourth smartest man in London, and that he just wanted to see the knees of his trousers. Afterwards they inspect the area and find a branch of the City and Suburban Bank in Aldersgate Street – a real bank, now part of the NatWest group. Holmes has basically now solved the case in this shortish early story (1891), perhaps a little disappointed that it was so easy, and at the end quotes Gustave Flaubert: 'L'homme, c'est rien – l'oevre, c'est tout'.

Proceed down Charterhouse Street to Smithfield Market. Meat has been sold here for 800 years. It was also the scene used for major medieval tournaments as well as public hangings for heretics – between 1400 and 1601, forty-three were hanged and six burned here – and others who had fatally fallen foul of the law. There once was a market for unwanted wives.

For Holmes' fans there is, on the southern side of Smithfield, St Bartholomew's Hospital, known as St Barts or just Barts, founded in 1123. In probably the most famous introduction in literature, young Stamford introduces Dr Watson to Sherlock Holmes in this building. They shake hands and Holmes says 'You have been in Afghanistan, I perceive.' Watson replies in astonishment: 'How on earth did you know that?' The stories are well and truly afoot; as a result of the meet-up, they are soon to begin sharing Mrs Hudson's rooms at 221B Baker Street.

The setting was used in the BBC *Sherlock* episode *The Reichenbach Fall* when Holmes, played by Benedict Cumberbatch has his final meeting with Moriarty, portrayed by Andrew Scott, on the roof of the hospital before jumping off to his supposed death.

Barts also has a very unusual museum, often referred to as 'weird' in an interesting sense, which houses surgical instruments, medieval manuscripts and paintings by William Hogarth. It is situated under the North Wing archway. Entry is free and it is open weekdays 10am to 4pm.

The location is an attractive one for writers. Charles Dickens, always with a keen eye for the dramatic and humorous, uses the great Smithfield area in *Oliver Twist*, *Great Expectations*, *Barnaby Rudge* and *Nicholas Nickleby*. Specifically regarding Barts, he chose the hospital as the place where the immortal Mrs Gamp in *Martin Chuzzlewit* has a friend who works as a nurse. In *Little Dorrit*, Arthur Clenham helps a wounded man into Barts where they see a surgeon. The injured man has been hit by a coach. The surgeon notes that the man's injuries are serious 'with the thoughtful pleasure of an artist contemplating the work on an easel…'

Before leaving, check for signs to the Museum of London, which charts the history of London from prehistoric to modern times. It is a wonderful museum, free to enter and fares very well on TripAdvisor. However, as it is currently 'on the move', best to check the latest status on museumoflondon.org.uk. Tel: 020 7001 9844.

The walk heads down Gresham Street towards Bank station, taking a right at Princes Street. Immediately before this, however, on the right, is Old Jewry and down here, at number 46, was the firm of Morrison, Morrison and Dodd. Holmes received a bizarre letter from them at the beginning of *The Adventure of the Sussex Vampire* letting them know that a Mr Robert Ferguson would soon be in touch on a matter concerning vampires. In this letter they mention Holmes' successful investigations in the matter of Matilda Briggs. Holmes tells Watson that Matilda Briggs is not a woman but a ship, which prompts a reference to one of the most famous untold stories in the canon as this ship is associated with the Giant Rat of Sumatra, a tale for which the world, says Holmes, is not yet prepared. This short mention has seen decades of speculation about the rat, a number of pastiches, plays, an album of music, a musical and even scholarly papers asking what kind of animal this giant rat could be. At the time of writing there is a report of a new species of giant rat, with very coarse fur, firm jaws and about the size of a well-fed cat, being located in Asia; is it possible that Conan Doyle in his youthful adventures on a whaling ship, came across such a creature? Undoubtedly, to the delight of Sherlockians everywhere, a great deal more along these lines will follow.

Conan Doyle was to write that throwing titles such as these fictitious cases about was to impress the reader with a general sense of power. In the same way and for the same reason, in the stories themselves he often has Holmes make clever deductions that have nothing to do with the matter in hand; he says that the South Americans apparently called these 'Sherlockolmitos'.

You will soon come to Bank tube station which has several exits, one of which is to a seated area fronted by the old Royal Exchange – which is now converted to cafes, offices and top-end shops – opposite the imposing edifice that is the Bank of England. This is much frequented by city workers, has seats, and is an excellent place to have a rest or eat your sandwiches while watching the comings and goings in this, the heart of the city's financial district.

The Bank of England was established in 1694 and was often referred to as 'The Old Lady of Threadneedle Street' after a satirical cartoon by James Gilray. Its main function was to act as the banker to the United Kingdom government although until 2016 employees could also hold personal accounts with it. Granted independence in setting monetary policy, the bank also now holds the gold reserves of the United Kingdom and thirty other countries in a vast underground vault. In 2020 the total value of the gold was £194 billion, enough, apparently, to cover the whole of the UK in gold leaf. There is a museum, free to enter, open on weekdays and very much worth a visit, the entrance of which is in Bartholomew Lane, off Threadneedle Street.

One of the most successful books of all time, *The Wind in the Willows*, was written after retirement by a Bank of England employee of thirty years, Kenneth Grahame. Conan Doyle would have been very much aware of it as publication was in 1908 and during the next twenty years the Edwardian adventures of Mole, Rat, Toad and Badger went through thirty printings. It has been adapted for stage and film, the latest being a musical written by Julian Fellowes in 2016.[43]

Holmesian locations within a short walking distance of Bank station

> 'After all, the best part of a holiday is perhaps not so much to be resting yourself, as to see all the other fellows busy working.'
>
> Kenneth Grahame, *Wind in the Willows*; as he worked here for three decades, Grahame probably had this area in mind when writing this

Using the present location as a base, there are several nearby Sherlockian addresses to see:

- The first couple are from a story which is set in this area called *The Stockbroker's Clerk*. It starts unusually in that Holmes drops in on Watson in his Paddington home and surgery and asks him if he fancies helping out with another case – today and in Birmingham. They are soon on a train and Holmes introduces Mr Hall Pycroft, 'a smart young City man', who until recently had a good job at Coxon and Woodhouse's of Draper Gardens. This location, at the corner of Throgmorton Avenue and Copthall Avenue, can be found just right off London Wall a short distance from where you are now. Also, just south of Bank station is Lombard Street which housed Mawson and Williams where young Pycroft at last manages to secure a good position, and which, unbeknown to him, he is destined never to take up. The story then moves to Birmingham before returning to Mawson and Williams for its shocking denouement.

- The next location of interest, leading off Bank station is Threadneedle Street. It is from the banking firm of Holder and Stevenson in this street that Alexander Holder arrives at 221B in a terrible funk regarding the fate of the Beryl Coronet, in an adventure of that name, the coronet being 'one of the most precious public possessions of the empire', in Watson's words.
- Then, in *The Man with the Twisted Lip* we find 'Hugh Boone', in reality Neville St Clair, selling wax vestas some 'little distance down Threadneedle Street' where there is 'a small angle in the wall'. Neville St Clair later admits 'that it was a very bad day in which I failed to take £2.'
- Finally, along Threadneedle Street, to the side of the Bank of England, is Bartholomew Lane and right at the top of this is Throgmorton Street. Mr James Dodd introduces himself to Holmes at the start of *The Adventure of the Blanched Soldier*, in a rare story written by Holmes himself and which he dates as happening in January 1903. Holmes reels off some facts about his guest: that he is from South Africa, in the Imperial Yeomanry and the Middlesex Corps. All this is correct and Mr Dodd is suitably impressed, calling Holmes a 'wizard'. Mr Dodd then begins his tale by saying that he is a stockbroker in Throgmorton Street.

The walk, when you are ready to leave the area of Bank, drops down to Cannon Street station, which has a mention in *The Man with the Twisted Lip* as it is from here that Mr St Clair habitually caught the 5.14 train to near Lee in Kent at the end of the working day (Conan Doyle was meticulous in planning the correct London mainline station for the travels of his characters; this route still operates except today it is the 5.39).

We then proceed to Monument tube, up Cornhill, and along Leadenhall Street to Aldgate tube. In *A Case of Identity*, Miss Mary Sutherland tells Holmes that her missing husband-to-be, Mr Hosmer Angel, had a position as a cashier 'in an office in Leadenhall Street', and she sent letters to him at Leadenhall Street Post Office

Nearby Aldgate station is central to the drama of *The Adventure of the Bruce-Partington Plans*, a matter serious enough to have Mycroft plead for his brother Sherlock's help. The top-secret plans for a submarine have gone missing when a young man, Cadogan West, is found on the tracks at Aldgate with some of the plans, but not the most vital ones, in his pocket. He has no ticket. Holmes, Lestrade and Watson visit the scene at Aldgate to begin piecing together the disparate parts of a strange puzzle which, as already mentioned in Walk 2, reaches a thrilling conclusion in Charing Cross Hotel. Among many highlights of the story is the telegram sent by Holmes, dining at Goldini's restaurant in Kensington, to Watson, asking him to come at once and making it quite clear that Holmes is proposing to break the law: 'Bring with you a jemmy, a dark lantern, a chisel, and a revolver.' The morality of Homes' actions is one thing, but there is always a ratcheting up of tension and excitement in the stories when such action is proposed, and especially if Watson is asked to bring a gun.

Leave Aldgate station and walk down Aldgate High Street which becomes Fenchurch Street a little farther on. Second on your left is Minories which features in *The Adventure of the Mazarin Stone* as the location of Straubenzee's workshop. Straubenzee is the master-maker of precision air guns, one of which Holmes believes is trained upon his dummy which he has set up in the window of 221B as he briefs Watson about Count Sylvius.

Back on the main road again, Lloyd's Register of Shipping is situated at 71 Fenchurch Street, which you will pass. Holmes is explaining to Watson, at the end of *The Five Orange Pips*, where he has been to finally tie up the complex case. 'I have spent the whole day,' said he, 'over Lloyd's registers and files of the old papers, following the future career of every vessel which touched at Pondicherry in January and February in '83'. One, the

Lone Star, caught Holmes' attention, but Holmes is not, for once, to have total satisfaction as the ship is lost in equinoctial gales in the Atlantic.

You may imagine, as you walk, a thriving fictitious firm – Westhouse and Marbank of Fenchurch Street – which was the wine importers that employed Miss Sutherland's stepfather, Mr Windibank, in *A Case of Identity* and was the source of the tickets to the gasfitters' ball where the lady met her fiancé, Mr Hosmer Angel. Unusually, when Holmes has revealed the true nature of the deception upon Miss Sutherland he declines to tell her, remarking to Watson: 'You may remember the old Persian saying, "There is danger for him who taketh the tiger cub, and danger also for who so snatches a delusion from a woman."'

Turn left into Mincing Lane – here was yet another imaginary firm, Ferguson and Muirhead, tea importers, created by Conan Doyle for the story *The Adventure of the Sussex Vampire*.

The walk is now near the Tower of London which is where, in *The Sign of Four*, Holmes tells Jones to head for in the police launch as they try to capture the *Aurora*. Specifically, he says to stop opposite Jacobson's Yard.

The walk ends here. Tower Hill tube is very close (District and Circle line) and the train will take you quickly back into the city centre. Hop on/hop off buses operate from here, too. Alternatively, you could cruise back along the river. Or, of course, stay for a while, see the Crown Jewels and explore the Tower along with the Thames riverside area.

If you travel any further east you will be in Whitechapel which is significant in that it was the area where Jack the Ripper operated and, in a Holmesian context, the setting for a large number of pastiches; writers have understandably been unable to resist the idea of combining Holmes and Jack the Ripper into a single story.

'The Weasel'

It was also the stamping ground of a character seen by many at the time as a real-life Sherlock Holmes – there are a few others, too, highlighted in other parts of this study. He was nicknamed 'The Weasel', not entirely kindly, and his name was Detective Inspector Frederick Porter Wensley (1865–1949). He was involved in solving the Houndsditch Murders and in the Siege of Sidney Street.

In December 1910 a group of Latvian immigrants attempted to rob a jeweller's in Houndsditch which resulted in the death of three policemen, the wounding of two others and the death of the leader of the gang, a man called George Gardstein. Most of the gang members were quickly rounded up but two escaped police until, on 3 January, they were holed up at 100 Sidney Street in Stepney. For the first time ever, as the police had inadequate weapons to deal with the danger, the army was called in and Winston Churchill himself controversially commanded the operation from the street. Pathe News filmed the stand-off which lasted six hours and resulted in the death of a fireman. The murdered policemen and fireman are today commemorated with plaques. The events have inspired novels and at least two films, *The Man Who Knew Too Much* (1934) and *The Siege of Sidney Street* (1960).

In a long and illustrious career DI Wensley was awarded both the King's Police Medal and the Order of the British Empire. He began his career in 1888 and retired in 1929, almost exactly the period when the public was accompanying Holmes on his many adventures and generally becoming more and more interested in criminal detection. His autobiography was originally called *Detective Days* but is better known by the title it assumed upon publication in America in 1931, *Forty Years of Scotland Yard*. He also kept a scrapbook of his many press cuttings, lovingly created by himself with scissors and glue, and which is preserved today at the Bishopsgate Institute.

WALKS AND TRIPS 8

Elsewhere in London; in the UK as a Whole

At A Glance – the following stories, plays and novels are highlighted in this chapter:

LONDON: north of the river: *The Stock-broker's Clerk. The Adventure of the Engineer's Thumb. The Boscombe Valley Mystery. Silver Blaze. The Adventure of the Red Circle. A Scandal in Bohemia. The Adventure of the Priory School. The Adventure of the Three Students.* **LONDON: south of the river:** *A Study in Scarlet. A Case of Identity. The Disappearance of Lady Frances Carfax. The Five Orange Pips. The Adventure of the Dying Detective. Micah Clarke. The Sign of Four.* **Berkshire:** *The Adventure of Shoscombe Old Place.* **Cambridgeshire:** *The Adventure of the Missing Three-Quarter. The Adventure of the Creeping Man. The Adventure of the Three Students.* **Cornwall:** *The Adventure of the Devil's Foot.* **Devon:** *Silver Blaze. The Hound of the Baskervilles. The Adventure of the Norwood Builder.* **Hampshire:** *The Adventure of the Cardboard Box. The Adventure of the Copper Beeches. The Problem of Thor Bridge.* **Herefordshire:** *The Boscombe Valley Mystery.* **Kent:** *The Adventure of the Golden Pince-Nez. The Adventure of the Abbey Grange. The Adventure of the Veiled Lodger.* **Midlands and North:** *The Adventure of the Stock-broker's Clerk. The Red-headed League. The Adventure of the Three Garridebs. The Adventure of the Priory School. The Adventure of the Copper Beeches.* **Norfolk:** *The 'Gloria Scott'. The Adventure of the Dancing Men. The Hound of the Baskervilles.* **Surrey:** *The Adventure of the Speckled Band. The Adventure of the Solitary Cyclist. The Five Orange Pips. The Reigate Puzzle.* **Sussex:** *The Adventure of Black Peter. The Adventure of the Second Stain. The Adventure of Wisteria Lodge. The Adventure of the Sussex Vampire. The Musgrave Ritual. The Adventure of the Lion's Mane*

London: north of the river

South Kensington is where Holmes and Watson sometimes go, if time and crime permit, to listen to opera. In *The Adventure of the Retired Colourman*, Holmes refers to music as a 'side door' by which to escape the wearying world and sets out to see Carina sing at the Albert Hall.

'Do you remember what Darwin says about music? He claims that the power of producing and appreciating it existed among the human race long before the power of speech was arrived at. Perhaps that is why we are so subtly influenced by it.'

A Study in Scarlet

The Adventure of Shoscombe Old Place opens with Holmes bent over a microscope and discussing the St Pancras case, which involved Merivale of the Yard. Holmes had provided crucial information by identifying zinc and copper filings in a man's cuff.

'Shortly after my marriage I had bought a connection in the Paddington district', Watson writes at the beginning of *The Stock-broker's Clerk*. One of the unusual features of the tale is that it is Holmes who goes to see Watson, rather than the other way around, after three months when they had seen little of each other. Holmes asks Watson if he is interested in a trip to Birmingham on a case, an offer that is enthusiastically accepted.

A year earlier – 1892 – Conan Doyle had also begun a tale at Watson's Paddington medical practice, in *The Adventure of the Engineer's Thumb*. We learn that Watson lived 'no very great distance from Paddington station' and sometimes received patients courtesy of the station staff; on this occasion a guard, 'my old ally', had brought a Mr Victor Hatherley, hydraulic engineer, who had had his thumb torn off. Watson suggests that they both take a cab to see Sherlock Holmes where, with the aid of the almost ubiquitous glass of brandy and water, Mr Hatherley explains his predicament which started when he took a train from Paddington station to Eyford in Berkshire.

There are a few other cases where a trip from Paddington station is required, one being at the start of *The Boscombe Valley Mystery* when Watson, sitting at breakfast with his wife, receives a telegram from Holmes asking that he come down by the 11.15 from Paddington. Another is in *Silver Blaze* when Holmes and Watson take a train from the station bound for King's Pyland in Dartmoor. The ensuing tale is especially interesting because Conan Doyle was never a 'man of the turf' and admitted that his ignorance was glaring. One sporting paper wrote a strongly worded critique of racing as depicted in the tale but this was OK because, although sometimes accurate details are essential, in this story they were not. The story, he declared, was 'alright'.

> 'There is nothing more deceptive than an obvious fact.'
>
> *The Boscombe Valley Mystery*

Hampstead features in three stories. In *The Adventure of the Red Circle*, Hampstead Heath is where Mr Warren comes to, having been mysteriously bungled from Tottenham Court Road (outside Morton and Waylight's, as mentioned in Walk 4) into a cab. It is also where Mr Hall Pycroft has his diggings – 17 Potter's Terrace – at the beginning of *The Stock-broker's Clerk*.

Most famously, perhaps, Appledore Towers is located here, the home of one of Holmes' most villainous foes, Charles Augustus Milverton: 'there are hundreds,' Holmes tells Watson, 'who turn white at his name.' Conan Doyle may have discussed this idea with his brother-in-law, E.W. Hornung, as a similar plot unfolds in the 1909 full-length novel *Mr Justice Raffles*. This novel bears another link to Sherlock Holmes as it marked the resurrection of Raffles due to public demand. Fans were divided in their opinion as the old carefree Raffles had now developed a darker side. It was filmed in 1977 with Anthony Valentine as Raffles, Christopher Strauli as Bunny Manders and a young Charles Dance as a cricketing friend. In this production, Raffles effectively murders an unscrupulous money lender in a most gruesome way – by setting his room and safe ablaze and locking the door by turning the key from the outside.

One of the most famous opening storylines in literature is 'To Sherlock Holmes she is always *the* woman.' This refers, of course, to Irene Adler who, in *A Scandal in Bohemia*, lives in Briony Lodge, Serpentine Avenue, St John's Wood. Unfortunately, if you try to pay a visit you will end up in Hyde Park; the avenue exists but not where Conan Doyle says it is. However, the general setting of the affluent St John's Wood is perfect for a mission undertaken by Holmes for the very grand-sounding Wilhelm Gottsreich Sigismond Von Ormstein, Grand Duke of Cassel-Felstein, hereditary King of Bohemia. That Holmes does not have everything go his way makes the story even more interesting.

The area is also home to Lord's Cricket Ground (nothing to do with the aristocracy, many people are surprised to learn, but named after its founder, Thomas Lord in 1814) in which Conan Doyle spent many happy hours as cricket was the sport which he said gave him most pleasure, something he shared with his brother-in-law and creator of the cricketing genius, Raffles, E.W. Hornung. Conan Doyle's greatest sporting feat, however – taking the wicket of the finest cricketer of the age, W.G. Grace – was in Crystal Palace although the incident when he was set on fire happened at Lord's: both are discussed in Part 1.

Perhaps surprisingly, cricket is barely mentioned in the canon – it is briefly referred to in *The Adventure of the Priory School* and *The Adventure of the Three Students* – but then again, neither is spiritualism, Conan Doyle's greatest interest in life.

A favourite of many, *The Adventure of the Six Napoleons* takes place in different parts of London including Kensington, Stepney, Kennington Road and Chiswick. The plot bears resemblances to *The Adventure of the Blue Carbuncle* in that a valuable gem has been hidden – in a bust of Napoleon here as opposed to a goose – and an exciting chase ensues to locate it. Lestrade is satisfyingly wrong all along and the ending sees Holmes at his dramatic best as he smashes a bust of Napoleon to reveal the famous black pearl of the Borgias. It is moving also to witness Lestrade's heart-felt praise of Holmes after the case is solved: 'We're not jealous of you at Scotland Yard. No, sir, we are very proud of you, and if you come down tomorrow, there's not a man, from the oldest inspector to the youngest constable, who wouldn't be glad to shake you by the hand'.

It is also famous for Holmes' reference to parsley sinking into butter, something that has launched hundreds of stories, pastiches and comedy sketches: 'You will remember, Watson, how the dreadful business of the Abernetty family was first brought to my notice by the depth which the parsley had sunk into the butter on a hot day.'

London: south of the river

Holmes' adventures take him south of the river sometimes, and one location which features often is the Camberwell area. In *A Study in Scarlet* it is the location of Madame Charpentier's boarding house – Torquay Terrace – and Sally Dennis' lodgings at 3 Mayfield Place, Peckham. Several other characters in the canon also live here; in *A Case of Identity*, the unfortunate Miss Mary Sutherland resides at 31 Lyon Place, Camberwell, as does Miss Dobney, governess, in *The Disappearance of Lady Frances Carfax*; most memorably, perhaps, Miss Mary Morstan, future wife of Dr Watson, shares a house with Mrs Cecil Forrester in Lower Camberwell.

The Camberwell poisoning case, mentioned at the start of *The Five Orange Pips*, is one of those cases that Watson says 'I may sketch out at some future date', along with adventure of the Paradol Chamber, of the Amateur Mendicant Society, the loss of the British barque *Sophy Anderson* and the singular adventures of the Grice Pattersons in the island of Uffa.

Rotherhithe is briefly mentioned in *The Adventure of the Dying Detective* as it is the perceived source of Holmes' terrible illness when he is apparently forced to take to his bed. The area has had a totally mixed history – once it was the northernmost part of the affluent county of Surrey; it was inhabited – and still is – by many people of Scandinavian descent; the Mayflower sailed from here to America in 1620, picking up people from Southampton en route; Conan Doyle mentions 'the cherry orchards at Rotherhithe' in *Micah Clarke* (1889) which is set in 1685; in Holmes' day it was an area of desperate poverty, while today it is being gentrified apace, helped by the extension of the underground system.

Among other areas south of the river and mentioned in the canon are Brixton, Croydon, Lee, Lewisham, Lower Norwood, Norbury, Beckenham, Penge and Streatham. The most famous use of this area, however, is in the very funny chase by Toby the dog in *The Sign of Four* when Holmes and Watson are led a merry dance in their pursuit of Jonathan Small: 'we had traversed Streatham, Brixton, Camberwell and now found ourselves in Kennington Lane....' They end up in Nine Elms before they both realise that the dog has been on a false trail upon which they both look blankly at each other before bursting simultaneously 'into an uncontrollable fit of laughter.'

Other Holmesian locations in the UK

Berkshire
The Adventure of Shoscombe Old Place is the last of the fifty-six short stories, first published in 1927 and centres around a stables in Berkshire. It is half horror and half detective story featuring a crypt, a hidden dead body, debt, a horse and a bizarre impersonation. It was originally to have been called *The Adventure of the Black Spaniel*. The Granada TV version features a very young Jude Law in a small but vital part; he was later to

play Watson to Robert Downey Jr as Holmes in controversial but popular and financially successful films of the tales. This 1991 TV production starring Jeremy Brett and Edward Hardwicke is seen as one of the most successful of the Granada series, using humour to great effect as a foil to the more grotesque aspects of the story.

Cambridgeshire

The Adventure of the Missing Three-Quarter was first published in 1904 and begins with the arrival of Mr Cyril Overton from Trinity College, Cambridge, who is seeking Holmes' help to locate a missing member of his rugby union team (the man who plays at the three-quarter position). It is, at the end, a sad tale as the missing man's wife has died of consumption. Rugby was one of Conan Doyle's favourite sports.

The Adventure of the Creeping Man is a tale first published in 1923. It takes place in Camford, a portmanteau of Oxford and Cambridge. It is a very powerful tale but has been dismissed by some as second-rate science fiction.

A 1904 tale, *The Adventure of the Three Students* is a simple and appealing tale where Holmes is set to find a cheating student. It is set in one of the great university towns in a college called St Luke's which, as above, sounds like it is part of Camford or Oxbridge.

Cornwall

The tale *The Adventure of the Devil's Foot* is set in Poldhu Bay, Cornwall, and is ninth in Conan Doyle's 'favourites' list. It is noteworthy as far as the present writer is concerned for several things. First, Holmes and Watson travel there because Holmes' usually iron health has broken and Dr Moore Agar of Harley Street orders a complete rest. Then it is unusually a horror story involving people being driven mad with suggestions of the supernatural. Third, Watson saves Holmes from almost certain madness or death by dragging him out of a room full of deadly fumes. Fourth, although this is not unique in the canon, it is a case where Holmes clearly operates outside the law – Holmes acts as police, judge and jury in letting the killer of Mortimer, Dr Sterndale, return to his work in Africa. Finally, it has Holmes comment on love: 'I have never loved, Watson, but if I did and the woman I loved had met such an end, I might act even as our lawless lion-hunter has done. Who knows?'

Conan Doyle would undoubtedly have known of Poldhu Bay as it was the location of Poldhu Wireless Station which in 1901, nine years before the story was published, was the location of Marconi's transmitter from which the first transatlantic radio message was sent.

Devon

Silver Blaze from *The Memoirs of Sherlock Holmes*, set in King's Pyland in Devon, was first published in 1892 and centres around the disappearance of a valuable horse. As discussed above, it is set in a world that Conan Doyle said he knew little about and one in which he had little interest. He said: 'I never could look upon flat racing as a true sport. Sport is what a man does, not what a horse does.' It has nonetheless become one of the most popular stories and usually features in the 'top 20' of all manner of surveys that constantly appear. It combines a mix of genuinely cruel skulduggery (mutilation of a horse's sinew) with the clever (using curry to disguise the taste of poison – in the Russian TV version this was substituted with a garlic sauce as this was more familiar to viewers) to the fantastical (disguising a horse from all who knew it by utilising dye). Holmes is assisted by one of the more efficient of official detectives, Gregory (except, of course, like all the others he lacks imagination). It also has one of Conan Doyle's most exciting and famous plot points as Holmes directs Gregory towards the curious incident of the dog in the night-time:

> Gregory: The dog did nothing in the night-time.
> Holmes: That was the curious incident.[44]

The first film version was in 1923 starring Eille Norwood as Holmes and Hubert Willis as Watson and at the time of writing can be seen on YouTube.

> 'Mr Holmes, they were the footprints of a gigantic hound!'
>
> Dr Mortimer, *The Hound of the Baskervilles*

Probably the most celebrated of the stories and one of the most famous ever written in the English language, *The Hound of the Baskervilles*, was first published in monthly instalments in *The Strand Magazine*. Set on the eerie and vast open space of Dartmoor, Conan Doyle said that his original idea was to produce a 'Victorian Creeper'. It was the first new Holmes adventure since his 'death' at Reichenbach and the public clamoured to get hold of it. Conan Doyle's American publisher had the idea of whetting people's appetite – not that this proved necessary – by putting a single isolated page of the tale up in bookshops and libraries; of the original approximately 195 sheets, only thirty-six are known to exist, each worth a fortune (one sold at auction in 2012 for $158,000).

The origins are disputed (see Part 1 for Norfolk's claim to fame here). A journalist, Bertram Fletcher Robinson, is sometimes credited with the original concept of a throat-ripping hound and is known to have explored Dartmoor with Conan Doyle. Bertram Fletcher, who wrote a series of his own featuring a detective called Addington Peace, undoubtedly developed a warm friendship with Conan Doyle, beginning on a ship during the long voyage from South Africa to Southampton, and certainly helped with the plot – he also contributed ideas to *The Adventure of the Norwood Builder* – but to what extent is still disputed.

An interesting aspect of the tale, given Conan Doyle's unshakeable belief in spiritualism, is the treatment of the supernatural element – is the hound a ghost-dog? In the story, many people are said to believe this, mainly the working class who are presented as not very bright (the believers, including at one point Watson himself who, as previously mentioned, Conan Doyle did not create to display imagination or humour) and it takes Holmes to prove that the tale belonged firmly in the here and now; the supernatural is debunked.

The book was immediately loved and received rave reviews from all and sundry, one national newspaper saying that it was a mix of a good melodrama and a skilful puzzle, that the excitement never flags from start to finish and that it would sharpen the wits of whoever read it.

There are literally hundreds of films and radio versions of the book, some plays and video games, and even a book arguing that Holmes got it wrong.[45] One of the most delightful ways it is used is by children and adults from all over the world who produce their own versions of part of it for artistic reasons or as a language-learning aid, and if you are a member of any of the Sherlock Holmes societies online you will see these pop up almost daily.

Hampshire

Conan Doyle's youthful adventures setting up a medical practice were in Southsea and it is not surprising that when he yearns for relief from a blazing hot summer that he thinks of the 'shingle of Southsea' at the start of *The Adventure of the Cardboard Box*.

> 'Crime is common. Logic is rare. Therefore it is upon the logic rather than upon the crime that you should dwell.'
>
> *The Adventure of the Copper Beeches*

The Adventure of the Copper Beeches is set five miles outside Winchester, the capital town of Hampshire and was first published in 1892, as usual in *The Strand Magazine*. It is an unsettling, melodramatic tale with a high 'horror' quotient. Miss Violet Hunter comes to Holmes as she has been offered an excessively generous salary to become a governess but she must agree to have her hair cut and, it subsequently emerges, to wear clothes provided by her employer and to sit in a certain window for various lengths of time. She is to be governess to a small boy with a penchant for cruelty and the other servants are chilly, one of them, Toller, is often drunk. A mastiff, kept hungry, roams the grounds at night. There is also a mysterious wing of the house, always locked. Holmes comes down and sorts out the mystery which involves money and a denied love affair.

It is hardly surprising that the story was selected in 1912 by Warner Features to become one of eight silent film adaptations which, as it says at the beginning of the film itself, was 'Produced under the personal supervision of the Author, Sir Arthur Conan Doyle.' It stars Georges Treville as Holmes (he wears a trilby hat, not the deerstalker as was later generally the case, and there is no Watson) and is viewable on YouTube; the whereabouts of all the others in the same series is unknown.

The Problem of Thor Bridge, one of the later stories first published in 1922, is set in a substantial estate in Hampshire and legal matters are subsequently dealt with in the Assizes in Winchester. It begins with the legendary declaration that there is a tin despatch-box with the name John H. Watson painted on it at the bank of Cox and Co, Charing Cross, which contains the notes to many cases, as yet unpublished, that had been investigated by Sherlock Holmes.

This statement is part of the conceit, also promoted by references to other tales (such as *The Giant Rat of Sumatra*, and see quote below under 'Kent') within the stories as they actually exist, that there is a wonderful world of more Holmes adventures 'out there somewhere'. Hundreds of pastiches inspired by this thought have been, and continue to be, written by everyone with a love for Holmes from schoolchildren as an essay assignment, to novels by celebrated authors such as Anthony Horowitz, whose two novels *The House of Silk* (2011) and *Moriarty* (2014) are exciting and highly regarded by Sherlockians.

The tale itself centres around the passion of unrequited love in which a suicide is designed to look like murder which simultaneously frames the rival in love. It involves an ingenious deception featuring a revolver, strong twine and a stone. Holmes demonstrates the mechanics of the suicide; this has been replicated using a fake gun by several groups of fans and it apparently 'works', which is not always the case in Conan Doyle's writings.

A 1968 adaptation starring Peter Cushing has mysteriously been lost. Elements from the tale were used in *You Do It to Yourself* (2012), written by Peter Blake in the first series of *Elementary*.

Herefordshire

In *The Boscombe Valley Mystery* (1891), although Holmes tells Watson that they are going to a country district near Ross in Herefordshire, to Boscombe Valley specifically, some Sherlockians are of differing opinions as to where the story takes place.

> 'Why does fate play such tricks with poor, helpless worms?'
>
> Sherlock Holmes, *The Boscombe Valley Mystery*

It is a tale of murder, greed and blackmail beginning in the Australian colonies, and is one more example of Holmes finding the killer only to keep the knowledge to himself, this time as the man is dying anyway and, as he tells him on release, 'will soon have to answer for your deed at a higher court than the Assizes.'

Kent

> As I turn over the pages, I see my notes upon the repulsive story of the red leech, and the terrible death of Crosby, the banker. Here also I find an account of the Addleton tragedy, and the singular contents of the ancient British barrow. The famous Smith-Mortimer succession case comes also within this period, and so does the tracking and arrest of Huret, the Boulevard assassin – an exploit which won for Holmes an autograph letter of thanks from the French President and the Order of the Legion of Honour.
>
> *The Adventure of the Golden Pince-Nez* (1904)

The ingenious tale, *The Adventure of the Golden Pince-Nez*, takes place near Chatham in Kent which associates itself particularly with Charles Dickens who lived a short distance away and featured several of the town's buildings in his novels.[46] Holmes solves the seemingly motiveless murder of young Willoughby Smith, cooperating with Hopkins from Scotland Yard. In the well-known Granada TV episode starring Jeremy Brett as Holmes, Watson is replaced by Mycroft and the plot differs slightly also (for example, instead of scattering cigarette ash on the floor in order to catch footprints of the murderer, Mycroft upsets his snuff box).

In *The Adventure of the Golden Pince-Nez*, both the professor and his estranged wife are Russian and both had, years previously, been involved with Nihilists. The rise of eastern gangs was the real-life backdrop against which Conan Doyle wrote this tale. There were an estimated 120,000 Jews alone, persecuted in Russia and elsewhere, who settled in England 1895–1914. Some of these were revolutionaries and formed into violent rival criminal gangs in parts of London, especially Whitechapel and the East End. Happenings such as the *Houndsditch Robbery* (see above), and the so-called *Tottenham Outrage* of 1909 when two self-proclaimed Russian revolutionaries attempted to rob a payroll van with the loss of two lives, stoked a xenophobia in sections of the population to which the Alien Act of 1905, which limited immigration, was in part a response.

The affluent area of Chislehurst is the setting for *The Adventure of the Abbey Grange* which once more sees Holmes partner with Inspector Hopkins to solve the murder of the odious Sir Eustace Brackenstall. Hopkins is, as you would expect, on the wrong scent altogether believing it to be part of a robbery-gone-wrong perpetrated by a local gang. The story is remarkable for the final scene in which Holmes acts as judge (this idea is discussed further in various parts of this book) and pardons the real murderer, Crocker. Here, however, he additionally involves Watson as the jury whose 'Not Guilty' verdict secures Crocker's release.

> 'Come, Watson, Come. The game is afoot.'
>
> *Adventure of the Abbey Grange*

Margate in Kent receives a mention in *The Adventure of the Veiled Lodger* when it is revealed that Leonardo drowned while bathing there. This is a late tale – 1927 – and quite bloody, notable additionally for Holmes' actions and kindness in saving someone – Mrs Ronder – from committing suicide.

Midlands and North
The Stock-broker's Clerk, set in London and Birmingham, was published in 1893. The primary feature of the plot – removing a man from his usual place of activity so that a crime can be committed – had previously been used by Conan Doyle two years earlier in *The Red-headed League* and was to be revived in 1924 for *The Adventure of the Three Garridebs*. The chap being deceived here, Mr Hall Pycroft, is a little brighter than his counterparts in the other two stories as he is suspicious from the outset and eventually understands the deception.

The Adventure of the Three Garridebs is also remarkable for the rarest of features – a display of emotion from Holmes and, at long last (it was written in 1924), an admission of the bond that existed for Holmes regarding Watson. We also learn that Holmes is quite prepared to commit murder if the cause (by his own standards, naturally) is justified. In the fight at the end, Watson is shot. Holmes crashes his gun onto the villain's head and begs Watson to say that he is not hurt. Watson tells the reader that it is worth a wound, many wounds, to have a glimpse of the love that lay behind Holmes' cold façade. Holmes then tells the assailant – Killer Evans – that he would not have got out of the room alive if Watson had been killed.

Holmes travels to Mackleton in the north east of England for *The Adventure of the Priory School* and ends up a very rich man, indeed, by accepting a cheque from the Duke of Holdernesse for £6,000. The reason he demanded this was undoubtedly at least partial annoyance at the Duke's attempt to deceive him, as normally he was not at all concerned with money and even waived fees altogether for deserving cases. The tale, with a fast-moving investigation spread over a vast and inhospitable terrain with a murder, strange animals and 'odd' locals, shares a similar excitement to *The Hound of the Baskervilles*, albeit at the other end of the country.

One other interesting aspect of the tale is that Conan Doyle says that he had many remonstrances about the impossibility of deciding which way a bicycle was heading by looking at the bicycle track upon a damp piece of ground, so many, in fact, that he took his own bicycle on to a similar stretch of ground to that featured in the story and had a look. He found that his correspondents were right; however, as the wheels made a deeper impression going uphill than down, Holmes was correct in his assumptions anyway.

Walsall in the West Midlands is the last place we hear of Miss Violet Hunter from *The Adventure of the Copper Beeches*, as Watson informs us at the last, in throw-away fashion, that she 'is now head of a private school at Walsall, where I believe she has met with considerable success'.

Detective Jerome: another candidate for a real-life Sherlock Holmes?

Jerome Caminada (1844–1914), often called 'Detective Jerome' by felons who found it difficult to pronounce his last name, has been called 'the real-life Sherlock Holmes'.[47]

His most famous case was *The Manchester Cab Murder* when 50-year-old John Fletcher was found slumped in a cab late at night, dying shortly afterwards. Although, when found, the victim had no money on him and his gold watch was missing, there was no sign of physical violence, the coroner pronouncing that he had died of alcohol and chemical poisoning – gin or beer mixed with choral hydrate, which was often taken to ward off sleep. Caminada, however, was able to further link chloral hydrate with the boxing community where it was used to drug fighters in order to fix the betting. A chain of clues involving a stolen bottle of the drug in Liverpool, a description of a young man from that area seen with the victim that night, and two victims who claimed to have been drugged in public houses before being robbed, led to the sensational arrest only three weeks after Fletcher's death, of 18-year-old Charlie Parton. The coup de grâce was locating a witness who actually saw Parton pour a substance from a phial into Fletcher's drink on the night in question. Parton was duly found guilty and sentenced to death, subsequently commuted to life imprisonment.

The above took place in the first half of 1889, when *A Study in Scarlet* had been out for just over a year, and it was all very Sherlockian. Immediately, the press began to refer to Caminada as 'Manchester's real-life Sherlock Holmes'. The parallels are striking – Caminada was brave, creative, extremely astute, not averse to using a gun if necessary, utilised a wide range of informers, and often went undercover; his results were also unprecedented – he is said to have sent 1,225 criminals to prison – and he was subsequently appointed Manchester's first CID superintendent. He retired in 1899 and became – among several other things including a Manchester City councillor – a private detective. He had no 'Boswell' or *Strand Magazine*, but he detailed his own exploits in two sets of memoirs, the first anonymously and the second under his own name, published in 1895 and 1901 – *Twenty-five years of Detective Life*, published in Manchester by the firm of John Heywood.

The 'Gloria Scott' is based in Donnithorpe, 'a little hamlet just to the north of Langmere, in the county of the Broads', and is chronologically the earliest of the stories, narrated by Holmes himself. It has been adapted in several forms, including being an episode in the animated series *Sherlock Holmes in the 22nd Century*, where the 'Gloria Scott', in the original a convict ship, becomes a spaceship travelling to the moon.

Conan Doyle liked to go motoring, a new and thrilling activity in the early 1900s, and this included trips around Norfolk, sometimes much to the terror of horses. Conan Doyle recounts one such trip down a narrow Norfolk lane when the horses pulling a cart-load of turnips panicked on coming into sight of his car – in which also sat his mother, knitting – and darted off up the bank. Conan Doyle rushed out to assist the furious farmer who was driving the cart and now saw his turnips all over the place. He looked back to witness his mother continuing to calmly knit. He writes that it was like a dream.

On one of the Norfolk motoring trips, he is reputed to have stayed at the Hill House Hotel in Happisburgh (pronounced 'Haisbro') and, while signing a lady's autograph book he saw some drawings by her children, Edith and Gilbert Cubitt, that seemed to be 'dancing men' and were, in fact, a coded language. The result was one of the most ingenious tales, *The Adventure of the Dancing Men*, parts of which he composed in the hotel. He uses the Cubitt name in the story. Norwich also features briefly as it is here that Abe Slaney is tried and found guilty of murder.

> 'I'm Sherlock Holmes and I always work alone 'cause no one can compete with my massive intellect.'
>
> > Watson, shouting out to Holmes in frustration as he tries in vain to gain entry to a crime scene in *The Blind Banker*, an episode in BBC's *Sherlock*. The production is based on *The Adventure of the Dancing Men*

Cromer's claim to fame, not universally accepted, as the possible inspiration behind *The Hound of the Baskervilles* is discussed in Part 1.

Conan Doyle also played golf in the region; the most famous club in the area is the Royal Sheringham Golf Club which at the time had a member named Moriarty.

Surrey

Conan Doyle's favourite story, discussed previously, *The Adventure of the Speckled Band* (1892), places the Roylotts in Stoke Moran, Surrey. *The Adventure of the Solitary Cyclist* (1903) is centred around Farnham: apparently it was initially rejected by *The Strand Magazine* as it had too much Watson and not enough Holmes, and Conan Doyle was never completely happy with it. At the time of its writing, Conan Doyle was living in Surrey, at 'Undershaw', which he had built specially to cater for his wife's health needs.[48]

The events of *The Naval Treaty* take place in Woking, north-west Surrey. This is a long story and was originally published in two parts. The conclusion sees Holmes at his theatrical best, the long-lost naval treaty being served up to a dumbfounded Percy Phelps and Watson at breakfast, literally on a platter. *The Adventure of Wisteria Lodge* sees Holmes travel to a house which is situated between Esher and Oxshott: Garcia had been found dead on Oxshott Common.

As he lived in the area for a long part of his life, it is perhaps surprising that Surrey does not feature more often in the canon; however, Portsdown Hill receives a mention in *The Five Orange Pips* and Watson's friend, Colonel Hayter, has a house in Reigate in *The Reigate Puzzle*.

Sussex
Sussex is used extensively by Conan Doyle. *The Adventure of Black Peter*, notable in part for featuring Stanley Hopkins, a detective regarded with respect by Holmes, is centred in Forest Row. The plot was used as the basis for the episode 'Dead Man's Tale' in the US series *Elementary*.

The macabre *Adventure of the Sussex Vampire* sees Holmes set off to Mr Ferguson's house in Sussex. It is in this tale that we hear of *The Giant Rat of Sumatra*, a tale for which the world is not yet prepared, and which has since inspired many pastiches.

The Manor House of Hurlstone in western Sussex is the scene of the solving of *The Musgrove Ritual*; T.S. Eliot adapted part of his 1935 play *Murder in the Cathedral* as homage to the tale.

The Adventure of the Lion's Mane is a later tale (1926), based in Sussex, and was highly rated by its author. It is unusual for several reasons: first, it is written by Holmes himself.[49] Conan Doyle later remarked that these stories were hampered by the absence of Watson's pen; second, it was published in *Liberty Magazine* in the United States prior to appearing in *The Strand Magazine* in the UK; third, it features no Watson at all; fourth, it is the only adventure set after Holmes' retirement,[50] and finally it is solved, not through Holmes' deductive powers, but his knowledge (of jellyfish).

Appendix I

A Timeline of the Stories

Number	Date	Story
1	Nov 1887	A Study in Scarlet
2	Feb 1890	The Sign of Four
3	Jul 1891	A Scandal in Bohemia
4	Aug 1891	The Red-headed League
5	Sept 1891	A Case of Identity
6	Oct 1891	The Boscombe Valley Mystery
7	Nov 1891	The Five Orange Pips
8	Dec 1891	The Man with the Twisted Lip
9	Jan 1892	The Adventure of the Blue Carbuncle
10	Feb 1892	The Adventure of the Speckled Band
11	Mar 1892	The Adventure of the Engineer's Thumb
12	Apr 1892	The Adventure of the Noble Bachelor
13	May 1892	The Adventure of the Beryl Coronet
14	June 1892	The Adventure of the Copper Beeches
15	Dec 1892	Silver Blaze
16	Jan 1893	The Adventure of the Cardboard Box
17	Feb 1893	The Yellow Face
18	Mar 1893	The Stock-broker's Clerk
19	Apr 1893	The 'Gloria Scott'
20	May 1893	The Musgrave Ritual
21	June 1893	The Reigate Puzzle
22	Jul 1893	The Crooked Man
23	Aug 1893	The Resident Patient
24	Sept 1893	The Greek Interpreter
25	Oct 1893	The Naval Treaty
26	Dec 1893	The Final Problem
27	Aug 1901–Apr 1902	The Hound of the Baskervilles
28	Sept 1903	The Adventure of the Empty House
29	Oct 1903	The Adventure of the Norwood Builder
30	Dec 1903	The Adventure of the Dancing Men

Appendix I 111

31	Dec 1903	The Adventure of the Solitary Cyclist
32	Jan 1904	The Adventure of the Priory School
33	Feb 1904	The Adventure of Black Peter
34	Mar 1904	The Adventure of Charles Augustus Milverton
35	Apr 1904	The Adventure of the Six Napoleons
36	June 1904	The Adventure of the Three Students
37	July 1904	The Adventure of the Golden Pince-Nez
38	Aug 1904	The Adventure of the Missing Three-Quarter
39	Sept 1904	The Adventure of the Abbey Grange
40	Dec 1904	The Adventure of the Second Stain
41	Aug 1908	The Adventure of Wisteria Lodge
42	Dec 1908	The Adventure of the Bruce-Partington Plans
43	Dec 1910	The Adventure of the Devil's Foot
44	Mar/Apr 1911	The Adventure of the Red Circle
45	Dec 1911	The Disappearance of Lady Frances Carfax
46	Nov 1913	The Adventure of the Dying Detective
47	Sept 1914 to May 1915	The Valley of Fear
48	Sept 1917	His Last Bow
49	Oct 1921	The Adventure of the Mazarin Stone
50	Feb/Mar 1922	The Problem of Thor Bridge
51	Mar 1923	The Adventure of the Creeping Man
52	Jan 1924	The Adventure of the Sussex Vampire
53	Oct 1924	The Adventure of the Three Garridebs
54	Nov 1924	The Adventure of the Illustrious Client
55	Sept 1926	The Adventure of the Three Gables
56	Oct 1926	The Adventure of the Blanched Soldier
57	Nov 1926	The Adventure of the Lion's Mane
58	Dec 1926	The Adventure of the Retired Colourman
59	Jan 1927	The Adventure of the Veiled Lodger
60	Mar 1927	The Adventure of Shoscombe Old Place

Appendix II

Some Notable Actors who have Played Holmes over the Years

The Arthur Conan Doyle Encyclopaedia puts the number of Holmes film adaptations since 1893 at over 1,200.[51]

There are literally dozens of actors who on radio, stage, TV and film, have portrayed the great consulting detective. Here are some of the most interesting for various reasons.

Regarding the filming of his tales, Conan Doyle wrote that films were in their infancy when Sherlock Holmes first appeared but he was pleased to sell the rights to a French company for a small sum – later, he had to buy the rights back at ten times the amount he had paid and regarded his original deal as a disastrous one. He was, however, delighted with the initial films by the Stoll Company with Eille Norwood as Holmes (see below), saying in his autobiography that the actor had 'that rare quality that can only be described as glamour'.

Tom BAKER
Tom Baker, later to play Doctor Who, was cast as Holmes in the four-part 1982 BBC mini-series, *The Hound of the Baskervilles*. Terence Rigby played Watson.

Jeremy BRETT
For many the quintessential Holmes, Jeremy Brett starred in the Granada TV series, *The Adventures of Sherlock Holmes*, from 1984 to 1994. It premiered on American television on 14 March 1985 on Mystery! Channel with Vincent Price as host. Brett had two Watsons in the series – David Burke and Edward Hardwicke. He remarked that Holmes was more difficult to play than *Hamlet*. His own mercurial moods reflected those that he saw in Holmes. He wanted to be the best Holmes ever.

Clive BROOK
Clive Brook (1887–1974) played Holmes in three movies, starting with the first 'talkie' Holmes movie, *The Return of Sherlock Holmes* in 1929. The final words of the film are perhaps the most famous ones that Holmes never said – 'Elementary, my dear Watson, Elementary'. He also played Holmes on radio and there is lively discussion about whether he, or William Gillette (see entry below), was the first here.

Sir Michael CAINE
Sir Michael Caine CBE played Holmes to Sir Ben Kingsley's Watson in *Without a Clue* (1988). In this much-heralded production, although at the time of release critics did not seem to share the fun, Watson is portrayed as the mastermind and Holmes a second-rate struggling actor who, when sober, does his best to remember the lines given to him. The film won *The Special Jury Prize* at the 1989 *Festival du Film Policier de Cognac*.

Henry CAVILL
In 2020 Henry Cavill played Holmes in the film Enola Holmes starring Millie Bobby Brown. The production is based on the work of novelist Nancy Springer, and follows Holmes and his younger sister, Enola. Helena Bonham Carter plays their mother. Reviews were generally favourable.

Peter COOK
Peter Cook played Holmes to Dudley Moore's Watson in the 1978 spoof of *The Hound of the Baskervilles*. It is included here as the worst-ever received film featuring Holmes and scored a 0 per cent rating on *Rotten Tomatoes*. This is even more remarkable as it is ablaze with comedic talent including Prunella Scales, Penelope Keith, Kenneth Williams, Roy Kinnear, Denholm Elliot, Irene Handl, Terry Thomas and Spike Milligan. Critics were merciless, especially given the high profile of all the leads. It was directed by Paul Morrisey, who also co-wrote the screenplay with Cook and Moore.

Benedict CUMBERBATCH
This portrayal, in the BBC's *Sherlock*, is probably responsible for bringing Sherlock Holmes fervour to millions of new, young fans, especially in Asia. Prime Minister David Cameron was famously asked at a Q and

A with young people in China, ostensibly political, if he could have the BBC hurry up and produce more episodes. The series, created by Mark Gatiss and Steven Moffat, starred Benedict Cumberbatch with Martin Freeman as Watson between (so far, as more episodes are often flagged up in the media) 2010 and 2017. The stories are set in the present day, notably of course in London, and modern-day equivalents are given for Conan Doyle's original features, for example, in the series, John Watson does not publish Holmes' exploits in print but on an online blog, and in his fight against tobacco Holmes uses nicotine patches – hence a 'three-pipe problem' becomes 'a three patch problem'.

Peter CUSHING

Peter Cushing played both Holmes and his creator, Sir Arthur Conan Doyle (*The Great Houdini* 1976). His initial film as Holmes was also the first of this famous tale to be made in colour – *The Hound of the Baskervilles*, 1959. He went on to play the detective in sixteen episodes of the BBC series *Sir Arthur Conan Doyle's Sherlock Holmes* (1965–68), most of which are now lost; the BBC had a policy of wiping and reusing tapes which may have a bearing here. His final outing as Holmes was in *The Masks of Death* (1984). He disliked Holmes as a very mercurial and arrogant man and remarked that he had to be careful not to annoy the audience in his portrayal; he also once famously remarked that he would rather have a job sweeping Paddington station than play him again.

Johnny DEPP

This actor was the voice of Holmes in the 2018 film *Sherlock Gnomes*. The film was generally critically panned, although it did make a modest profit worldwide on its $65 million budget. *Rotten Tomatoes* website said that the greatest mystery about the film was why it existed at all.

Robert DOWNEY Jr

Robert Downey Jr first played Holmes, alongside Jude Law as Watson in the 2009 film *Sherlock Holmes*, directed by Guy Ritchie. It was followed in 2011 by *Sherlock Holmes: A Game of Shadows*. At the time of writing, a third film is scheduled, to be directed by Dexter Fletcher. Both films so far have been critical and commercial successes, although some fans see the films as more a series of action-packed stunts than homage to the canon. The 2009 film was nominated for two Academy Awards, Best Original Score and Best Art Direction.

Rupert EVERETT
Rupert Everett played Holmes in the 2004 TV film *Sherlock Holmes and Case of the Silk Stocking*, with Ian Hart as a sprightly Watson, married to an American psychoanalyst. Everett plays Holmes as an elegant, masterful character, with some flashes of decadence and camp. The film gained mainly positive reviews.

Stephen FRY (audio)
The pairing of Holmes and Stephen Fry, who is a lifelong Sherlockian and has recorded the entire canon, was described by *The New York Times* as a marriage made in heaven – one national treasure reading the adventures of another. The reason for Holmes' continuing popularity, the same paper suggests, is that he restores order to a world that we often find incomprehensible.

Dean FUJIOKA
Voted Japan's sexiest man in 2017, Dean Fujioka plays Holmes in the highly praised and entertaining series *Sherlock: Untold Stories*. Takanori Awata is Watson. Holmes is hugely popular in Japan – you can visit a Holmes-themed bar in Ikebukuru.

William GILLETTE
William Gillette (1853–1937) was an American actor who created the first great defining Holmes. He played Holmes over 1,300 times, incorporating the deerstalker hat – originally 'added' by the legendary illustrator, Sidney Paget in *The Strand Magazine* – and changing a straight pipe to a curved one, possibly because this allowed him to articulate his lines better and it also did not obscure his face from the audience. He also included in the production a magnifying glass, syringe and violin.

After 'killing off' Holmes, Conan Doyle found himself in need of money, especially as he was about the build his new house, 'Undershaw'. Holmes had already appeared on stage a couple of times, but he wrote a brand new five-act play. He offered the part of Holmes firstly to Herbert Beerbohm Tree and then to Henry Irving, both of whom declined. The play was then rejigged involving several people, Conan Doyle going along with this quite happily, the only proviso being that there should be no love interest for Holmes. Gillette then came into the writing picture, famously asking Conan Doyle if he could 'marry' Holmes, to which came the reply: 'You may marry or murder or do what you like with him'. The result was a four-act play, *Sherlock Holmes*, largely based on *A Scandal in Bohemia* and *The Final Problem*, but also incorporating elements and complete passages of dialogue from other parts of the canon. The resulting production opened in Buffalo USA before transferring to Broadway and then to the Lyric Theatre in London. Despite some sniffy critical reviews, the production was a gigantic financial success, the run at the Lyric alone making Gillette an estimated £100,000.

Between 1914 and 1919 Gillette spent over a million dollars on building Gillette Castle in Hadlyme, Connecticut; it had towers, turrets and a 3-mile miniature railroad (by which means the stone for building work had been carried). The castle and grounds eventually transferred to state ownership and has had $11 million dollars spent on it since 2002; it is currently one of the top three tourist attractions in Connecticut. As you might expect, there is some Sherlock Holmes memorabilia to be seen here. At the time of writing, the site is overwhelmingly rated five stars on TripAdvisor www.tripadvisor.co.uk.

Stuart GRANGER

Stewart Granger starred opposite Bernard Fox as Watson and William Shatner as George Stapleton in a made-for-TV American colour film of *The Hound of the Baskervilles* in 1972. Reviews were appalling and the original idea of further films featuring other detectives was dropped.

Charlton HESTON

The play *The Crucifer of Blood*, written by Paul Giovanni and based loosely on *The Sign of Four* ran for just over a month in Los Angeles from December 1980 to mid-January 1981. It starred Charlton Heston as Holmes and, intriguingly considering what was to happen a few years later, Jeremy Brett as Watson (see Jeremy Brett above).

Ronald HOWARD

The son of actor Leslie Howard (whose plane was mysteriously shot down in 1943, deliberately targeted, Ronald believed, by the Nazis possibly because his father had made fun of Goebbels in a film). In the 1980s he wrote *In Search of My Father: A Portrait of Leslie Howard* in which he explores the shooting down of the aircraft in detail. Ronald Howard has a special place in many Sherlockian hearts for the thirty-nine episodes of *Sherlock Holmes,* made in 1954, in which he starred opposite Howard Marion-Crawford as Watson. The Director was the American TV producer Sheldon Reynolds (1923–2003), who was to produce another, though less successful, series in 1979, *Sherlock Holmes and Doctor Watson.* The last DVD release of the 1954 series was in 2014.

Christopher LEE

Christopher Lee (1922–2015) made several contributions to the canon both as an actor and narrator. He began by playing Sir Henry Baskerville in *The Hound of the Baskervilles* in 1959 (with Peter Cushing as Holmes). He played Holmes himself in *Sherlock Holmes und das Halsband des Todes* (Sherlock Holmes and the Deadly Necklace) in 1962 and, thirty years later, *Sherlock Holmes and the Leading Lady* and *Incident at Victoria Falls,* both of which received middling reviews although Lee's performance was praised. He also played Mycroft Holmes in the 1970 production, *The Private Life of Sherlock Holmes.* In 1985 he was the narrator of the TV documentary, *The Many Faces of Sherlock Holmes.*

Vasily LIVANOV

Sherlock fans who discover the Russian-made *The Adventures of Sherlock Holmes and Dr Watson* (1979–86) generally agree that the series is a rich delight. While the settings, such as Baker Street which is actually a street in Riga, Latvia, and many others, bear little resemblance to London and the inside of 221B is quite dark containing many heavy wooden pieces of furniture that you cannot imagine Mrs Hudson tolerating or cleaning, the actual stories stay very faithful to the original texts. Holmes is played by Vasily Livanov and Watson, as a very able man, by Vitaly Solomin; the two have a light and easy chemistry between them. Some changes were necessary to satisfy the Russian censor, for instance, Holmes' cocaine use is never mentioned. The show was an enormous success on Russian television and today can be bought on DVD with English subtitles. Livanov's wax statue sits today inside 221B Baker Street.

Henry LLOYD-HUGHES

This actor, who appeared in *Harry Potter and the Goblet of Fire* (2005) is cast as Holmes in *The Irregulars* which, at the times of writing, is being produced by Netflix. Royce Pierreson is Watson.

Maksim MATVEYEV

Matveyev stars as Holmes in a new Russian TV production based on the works of Conan Doyle, the third so far, titled *Sherlock Holmes in Russia*. His first film was *Vice* in 2007, since which he has starred in many. He was made 'Honoured Artist of the Russian Federation' in 2018.

Sir Ian McKELLEN

McKellen plays Holmes in the fine and unusual study *Mr Holmes* (2015) which sees a 93-year-old Holmes living in retirement, battling to solve one last case as his mind deteriorates. Laura Linney and Milo Parker excel alongside McKellen at the peak of his powers. It gained 86 per cent on Tomatometer (*Rotten Tomatoes*) and gives us another version of Holmes, far more subtle and human than most.

Jonny LEE MILLER

Another actor, and friend of Benedict Cumberbatch, who portrayed Holmes in the present day, but this time working around Manhattan in the CBS series *Elementary*, beginning in 2012 and running seven seasons until 2019. Dr Watson is played by Lucy Liu. As there were twenty-four episodes per season, Jonny Lee Miller became at the end of season two, technically at least, the actor to have played Holmes more than any other. Holmes is portrayed as a recovering drug addict 'exiled' by his wealthy father to a large brownstone which he shares with Dr Joan Watson, hired by his father as a sober companion. Lee Miller has said that, for him, the shifting and developing friendship between Holmes and Watson is a key element.

Sir Roger MOORE

Many people's favourite James Bond also makes a decent fist of playing the great consulting detective opposite Patrick Macnee (Steed in *The Avengers*) and Charlotte Rampling as Irene Adler, in *Sherlock Holmes in New York* (1976). Here, they battle Professor Moriarty as the 'Napoleon of Crime' tries to pull off the ultimate bank robbery. At the end of the film, a clear suggestion is left with the audience that Irene Adler's son was fathered by Holmes (the child is uncommonly bright and Irene Adler gives Holmes a picture of him to keep). Macnee, in this film playing a bumbling Dr Watson, was to subsequently play a much more astute character alongside Christopher Lee's Holmes (see entry above). Moore, as James Bond, and Macnee, as Sir Godfrey Tibbett, were to team up again, having enormous fun, in *A View to a Kill* (1985).

Eille NORWOOD

Anthony Edward Brett (1861–1948) used the stage name Eille Norwood, reputedly in part tribute to a woman he loved called Eilleen and also as he lived in Norwood, south London.

Eille Norwood played Holmes in forty-seven silent films (forty-five were shorts) between 1921 and 1923. He also played Holmes in a stage play *The Return of Sherlock Holmes* in 1923. Conan Doyle called his interpretation 'wonderful'.

Peter O'TOOLE

Peter O'Toole voiced four animated productions for Australian television in 1983, one of which was *The Hound of the Baskervilles*. Peter O'Toole was nominated for an Academy Award eight times without winning.

Igor PETRENKO

A new Russian TV series *Sherlock Holmes* was aired in 2013 starring Igor Petrenko as a 27-year-old Holmes and Andrei Panin as Watson, an ex-army doctor some fifteen years older. They meet and both subsequently live in cramped and grimy rooms in central London. In this production Holmes is terrible at the violin. The production was generally welcomed. Sadly, Andrei Panin died before completing the eight episodes that make up the series but left sufficient material for the editors to finish the production.

Tim PIGOTT-SMITH

Tim Pigott-Smith (1946–2017) played Watson in William Gillette's (see entry above) play *Sherlock Holmes* on Broadway, New York 1974–5. John Wood was Holmes. In 1986 he recorded *Valley of Fear* for BBC Radio in which he played Holmes opposite Andrew Hilton as Watson. He also wrote three children's book featuring The Baker Street Irregulars: *The Dragon Tattoo* (2008), *Shadow of Evil* and *Rose of Africa* (both 2009).

Christopher PLUMMER

Murder by Decree was a 1979 joint UK/Canadian production, starring Christopher Plummer as Holmes alongside James Mason as Watson, and directed by Bob Clark. The plot, devised by John Hopkins who also wrote the script for the James Bond film *Thunderball*, centres around the Jack the Ripper killings. The reviews were greatly mixed.

Basil RATHBONE

The fourteen films starring Basil Rathbone, supported by a bumbling Watson played by Nigel Bruce (1939–46) are evidence that *Sherlock* and *Elementary* were not the first attempts to transfer Holmes to a different era. At the start *of Sherlock Holmes and the Voice of Terror* (1942) we are told that Holmes is 'ageless, invincible and unchanging', as he goes into battle with the Nazis. Rathbone, apparently selected for the role at a Hollywood party, became the definitive Holmes, elegant, quick-witted and omniscient, for a generation before tiring of the part by 1946.

Ian RICHARDSON

Ian Richardson CBE (1934–2007) played Holmes in two 1983 TV films, *The Sign of Four* and *The Hound of the Baskervilles*. The two films were shot simultaneously. The American producer Sy Weintraub, famous at the time as the force behind the Tarzan films of 1959–68, did not realise that Granada were about to film the now famous series starring Jeremy Brett and, after he found out and following complicated legal manoeuvres, abandoned his plan to film more stories.

Nicholas ROWE

Nicholas Rowe (born 1966) came to fame very early in his career in the 1985 production of *Young Sherlock Holmes*, reading for the part while still at school. Thirty years later he also appeared as Holmes in a film that Ian McKellen (see entry above) goes to see in the cinema in *Mr Holmes* (2015). *Young Sherlock Holmes* gained mixed reviews with some seeing the swashbuckling style as 'Sherlock Holmes meets *Raiders of the Lost Ark*' (a film by Steven Spielberg 1981). It just recouped the production budget of $18 million.

Sir Robert STEPHENS

Sir Robert Stephens (1931–95), acclaimed by many as the greatest actor of his generation, was a confirmed Holmesian and starred in Billy Wilder's *The Private Life of Sherlock Holmes*, opposite Colin Blakely as Watson, in 1970. Christopher Lee (see entry above) played Mycroft Holmes. There was deliberate and melancholy ambiguity about Holmes' sexuality and his exact relationship with Watson. Mark Gatiss and Steven Moffat, the creators and writers of the BBC's *Sherlock*, have quoted the film as an inspiration. Critical reception was generally positive. In his 2002 review of the film, Peter Bradshaw describes Stephens' Holmes as 'splendidly debonair'.

Yuko TAKEUCHI

Yuko Takeuchi stars as Sara 'Sherlock' Shelly Futaba and Shihori Kanjiya as Dr Wato Tachibana in an all-female take on Holmes and Watson, *Miss Sherlock,* an eight-episode series set in Japan and released in 2018. This is the first major production based on Sir Arthur Conan Doyle's original characters where both leads are women. At the time of writing, the future of the series is under review.

Geoffrey WHITEHEAD

Sherlock Holmes and Dr Watson was the name given to a relatively obscure 1979 production starring Geoffrey Whitehead as Holmes, Donald Pickering as Watson and Patrick Newell as Lestrade. It was made on a low budget in Poland and directed by Sheldon Reynolds. It has an enthusiastic fan base as a cult classic, partly because the leads play very well off each other and partly for its humour but it was, unfortunately, hit by post-production issues which meant that the series was never released in the UK. There were twenty-four episodes.

Nicol WILLIAMSON
The Seven-Per-Cent Solution was a ground-breaking 1976 production based on Nicholas Meyer's 1974 novel of the same name. The author also scripted the film. It starred Nicol Williamson as Holmes, Robert Duval as Watson, Alan Arkin as Freud and Sir Laurence Olivier as Professor Moriarty. Holmes is tricked into going to Vienna to consult Sigmund Freud as Watson fears he is dangerously unstable; it is this departure from the almost omniscient character portrayed by actors up to Rathbone that has led many critics to see this film as the forerunner of the more twitchy, moody-but-brilliant Holmes played notably by Benedict Cumberbatch (BBC's *Sherlock*) and Jonny Lee Miller (CBS' *Elementary*). The American press was most impressed with the film, the British press less so. It received two Academy Award nominations, for Best Writing and Best Costume Design.

Douglas WILMER
Douglas Wilmer (1920–2016) was an actor noted for playing Holmes in the 1965 series *Sherlock Holmes*. Nigel Stock played Watson. He was a lifelong fan of the canon and, to criticism from some, played Holmes as an unsympathetic character, declaring it would have been 'hell' to share rooms with him. The series was very favourably received by viewers. In 2012 he made a cameo appearance in the final episode of the BBC production of *Sherlock*. He had various Sherlockian aspects to his life which included running a wine bar called 'Sherlocks' in Woodbridge, Suffolk, in the 1980s. In 1991 he was elected an Honorary Member of the Sherlock Holmes Society of London and in 2000 the Baker Street Irregulars awarded him the Irregular Shilling. He died aged 96 on 31 March 2016.

Arthur WONTNER
Before being cast as Sherlock Holmes in 1931, Arthur Wontner had already played many stage roles, including Bunny Manders in *Raffles, The Amateur Cracksman* (see Walk 6), and Sexton Blake, a character derived from Holmes. Of the five films in which he played Holmes, one – *The Missing Rembrandt* – is lost. Some love his performances, seeing them as satisfyingly solid, but he is often referred to as 'the forgotten Holmes', as shortly afterwards Basil Rathbone was to make the role his own for many years.

Appendix III

An Alphabetical Sherlock Holmes Miscellany

BIRTH. Sherlock Holmes may have been born in 1854; the reason for this is that in *His Last Bow*, published in 1914, he is described as a man of 60 years of age. The great Sherlockian scholars, Christopher Morley and William Baring-Gould have further refined this to give him a birthday of 6 January. He has a brother, Mycroft, elder by seven years. We gain few clues as to his lineage except that he says his ancestors were country squires and that his grandmother was sister to the French artist Vernet.

BUDDHIST ENLIGHTENMENT. Some believe Holmes to still be alive because: 1) He spent some time with the chief Lama in Tibet during the Great Hiatus and gained Buddhist enlightenment: this would account for his returning in the hours of our greatest peril, e.g. during the Second World War, or in the present day – witness BBC's *Sherlock* or CBS' *Elementary* which are seen as indications by some that he is here – as enlightened beings are not bound by laws of life and death. It has also been pointed out that he practises mindfulness which is a key Buddhist concept. 2) His death has never been reported in *The Times* newspaper.

CONSULTING DETECTIVE. Sherlock Holmes refers to himself as the world's only Consulting Detective, a role he invented. C. Auguste Dupin, created by Edgar Allan Poe, appeared in what is usually seen as the first ever detective story, *The Murders in the Rue Morgue*, in 1841.

DISGUISES. Holmes has a flair for the theatrical and is an expert in disguises. Among the most memorable are a sailor in *The Sign of Four*; an old Italian priest in *The Final Problem* (see Walk 2); and a doddering bookseller in *The Adventure of the Empty House* (see Walk 3).

DRUGS. Holmes sometimes uses drugs, especially if he has no stimulating case on which to work. Sometimes this is morphine and at others, cocaine, which he injects in a 7 per cent solution. Both drugs were legally obtainable when the stories were written. Both Watson and Holmes smoke cigarettes, cigars and pipes, but Watson does not consider this a vice.

ELECTRIC LOCOMOTIVE. Sherlock Holmes had an electric locomotive named after him in the 1920s by the London Metropolitan Railway. The Metropolitan is one of the underground lines serving Baker Street Tube station today.

FANDOM. The idea of fandom, a way of life incorporating extreme interest in a person, group or character has been significantly influenced by Holmes, beginning, perhaps, in 1893 when, upon 'killing off' Sherlock Holmes, Conan Doyle was responsible for 20,000 people cancelling their subscription to *The Strand Magazine*.

FEES. The fee that Conan Doyle received for *A Study in Scarlet* in 1887 was just £25. By the dawn of the new century, however, he was one of the world's wealthiest men of letters.

The fees Holmes charges are generally on a fixed scale, except when he either waives them altogether, or charges more to clients who are wealthy and/or, by his reasoning, deserving of a financial lesson – he charges the Duke of Holderness £6,000 in *The Adventure of the Priory School*.

GREAT HIATUS. The period May 1891 – April 1894, when everyone, including Watson, thought Holmes was dead is referred to as the Great Hiatus.

HUMAN CHARACTER (MOST PORTRAYED). Holmes is, according to Guinness World Records, the most portrayed human character in literary history; depictions by means of film, audio and theatre run into the tens of thousands and show no signs of slowing today. The stories are available in seventy languages.

HONOURS. In terms of Honours, Holmes received the Legion of Honour in 1894 for the tracking down of Huret, the Boulevard assassin in Paris. He refused a knighthood. In 2002 he was awarded an honorary fellowship of the Royal Society of Chemistry, the only fictional character ever thus honoured.

HUMAN MEMORY. Holmes believes that the capacity for human memory is finite, that you can indeed fill up your head with non-essential things. That is why he astonishes Watson by not knowing that the earth revolves around the sun. Conan Doyle changes this as the stories progress, probably to make Holmes a more rounded and interesting character study.

KNOWLEDGE. Watson makes an assessment of Holmes' knowledge shortly after meeting him in *A Study in Scarlet*. Briefly, the situation is as follows: Literature, Philosophy and Astronomy – nil; politics – feeble; Botany – variable, well up on belladonna, opium and poisons but knows nothing of everyday gardening; Geology – practical but limited, can easily tell different soils from each other; Chemistry – profound; Anatomy – practical; Sensational Literature – immense, he knows 'every detail of every horror' perpetrated in the last century; British Law – good practical knowledge.

MIDDLE NAME OF WATSON. Dr Watson's middle name is unknown. The initial is 'H', but nowhere in the canon is the name given. Favourite guess is probably 'Hamish', which Dorothy L. Sayers (1893–1957) liked to think; this is also given as his middle name by Watson in the BBC production of *Sherlock*.

PARODIES. Parodies are humorous stories where the names of Holmes and Watson, or the title of the tales, are often changed for comic effect. J.M. Barrie wrote a short parody, *My Evening with Sherlock Holmes* (*Speaker Magazine*, 28 November 1891), in which the writer, annoyed that Sherlock Holmes is receiving so much attention, resolves to spend an evening getting the better of him; it involves a very funny exercise in what can be deduced from Sherlock Holmes' hat. The parodies over the next few years included the following: *The Adventures of Sherwood Hoakes* (1892); *The Adventures of Shylock Oames* (1892); *The Adventures* of *Chubblock Homes* (1893); *The Adventures of Picklock Holes* (1894); *The Adventure of the Tomato on the Wall* (1894); *The Recrudescence of Sherlock Holmes* (1894); *The Sign of the '400'* (1894); *The Genius of Herlock Sholmes* (1895); and *The Cat of the Bunkervilles* (1902).

PASTICHES. A pastiche is defined as an artistic work in the style of another, and there are very many Sherlock Holmes pastiches. The first was by Conan Doyle's friend, J.M. Barrie. It was called *The Late Sherlock Holmes* and was published in 1893. The tradition of the pastiche has continued to this day. Conan Doyle's son, Adrian, wrote twelve original stories, *The Exploits of Sherlock Holmes*.

SHERLOCK HOLMES DAY. There is a Sherlock Holmes Day – 22 May. It was first celebrated in 2019 and was chosen simply because it is Sir Arthur Conan Doyle's birthday. The same day is also apparently Nutty Fudge Day.

WATSON'S WAR WOUND. Watson's war wound is one of the mysteries of the canon. When we first meet him (and he first meets Sherlock Holmes) we are told that his left arm has been injured and that he holds it in a stiff and unnatural way. In the very next story, *The Sign of Four*, Watson sits nursing his wounded leg because, 'I had a Jezail bullet through it sometime before.' As with other areas of the canon, theorists have been at work. Some have gone to great lengths to work out a number of ways Watson could have been sitting, standing or perhaps tending to a patient where a single bullet could have caused both injuries. The most extreme idea is that Watson was killed and that his orderly, Murray, whose bravery he says saved him when shot, took his identity; the subsequent guilt accounts for this and other confusions about his life, including whether he was called 'James' or 'John'.

> 'How often have I said to you that when you have eliminated the impossible, whatever remains, however improbable, must be the truth?'
>
> *The Sign of Four*

WOMEN AND HOLMES. Holmes' attitude to women is more complex than often presented. He thought that being married would affect his judgement and the one thing that Conan Doyle forbade when writers asked if they could adapt his plays is a 'love interest' for Holmes. He looks remarkably infatuated with Irene Adler, though, in *A Scandal in Bohemia*. He can be very charming, which is one reason Mrs Hudson tolerates him as a tenant. Also, in *The Adventure of Charles Augustus Milverton* he rapidly becomes engaged to a maid, only to vanish when she can no longer be of use in gaining information for him.

Notes

1. This is how Conan Doyle introduces Holmes in *Memories and Adventures*. He said that the character permitted no light or shade as adding anything to a man who was basically a calculating machine would lessen his impact; he was sometimes inclined to weary of him for this reason.
2. Conan Doyle probably had one of two characters in mind here. In *David Copperfield* he is first sent to learn under the dreadful and often drunk Mr Creakle, who puts a sign around David's neck which reads 'Take care of him. He bites'. It is only removed as it gets in the way of beatings. The other candidate, Thomas Gradgrind, in *Hard Times*, is the cold and unfeeling school superintendent who, at least when we first meet him has no time for emotion, declaring: '*Facts* alone are wanted in life. Plant nothing else, and root out everything else.'
3. The almost eleven-minute interview is at the time of writing available on YouTube.
4. More parody titles are given in Appendix 3: An Alphabetical Sherlock Holmes Miscellany.
5. See Appendix 2 for more information on William Gillette.
6. Conan Doyle played ten first class matches, mainly for Marylebone Cricket Club. He was a useful slow bowler and competent lower-order batsman. In eighteen first class innings he averaged 12.8 with a top score of 43.
7. 'You should have gone to Cromer, my dear, if you went anywhere. Perry was a week at Cromer once, and he holds it to be the best of all sea-bathing places. A fine open sea, he says, and very pure air.' (advice from Mr Woodhouse)
8. If you are using buses and underground trains (the 'tube') you can buy tickets as you go; you can buy a daily pass (no travel before 0930); or, probably most convenient and cheapest, you can buy an 'oyster card' (travel anytime). This may require some simple planning in advance in order to receive one https://oyster.tfl.gov.uk/ As regards accommodation, London is very expensive and an excellent and cost-effective alternative to hotels are university rooms, available when students are on vacation www.universityrooms.com.
9. Interview currently on YouTube – see note 3 also.
10. website Ihearofsherlockeverywhere.com.
11. There are also two other 'stories', both very short. *The Field Bazaar* was written in 1896 in order to help raise money for a cricket pavilion on ground purchased by Edinburgh University. It was published in *Student* and is

simply an analysis by Holmes of what Watson was thinking at breakfast. It begins with the words, 'I should certainly do it.' The other is *How Watson Learned the Trick*, which is a very funny take of the same subject and was published by Methuen in 1924.

12. 221B Baker Street is one of the most famous addresses in the world, especially considering that it never actually existed. A great many people have had fun with the number and here are a few examples. In 1987 CBS made a movie, *The Return of Sherlock Holmes* (not to be confused with many others of that name), in which Holmes is cryogenically frozen and returned to life over a hundred years later; on searching for his old home he finds it turned into a McDonalds hamburger franchise. In the hugely successful American TV series *House M.D.*, Dr Gregory House lives in 221 Baker Street, Apartment B, Princeton, USA. In the wonderful 2015 movie *Mr Holmes*, starring Sir Ian McKellen, we see Holmes looking out from the real 221B to a house surrounded by tourists and fans on the opposite side of the street and he remarks that Watson had deliberately given the wrong location in his stories.

The interior of the flat has been recreated in many places around the world, including at Meiringen, Switzerland, near the Reichenbach Falls, where the windows were shipped over from England and the wallpaper copied from an authentic late nineteenth-century pattern. There is another recreation in a hotel in Lucens and in the library of the University of Minnesota, USA. Some artefacts and furniture can also be seen in the Sherlock Holmes pub (see Walk 2).

As regards the address itself, some see it as a typical English townhouse divided into flats and 221B as one of these. A good deal of creative brainpower has been used over the years to try to answer the question: 'If Sherlock Holmes lived at 221B Baker Street, then who lived at 221A?' It could, of course, be Mrs Hudson and an attempt at answering this question is in the BBC production of *Sherlock* (2010–17) when the viewer is taken to a flat in the basement of 221B that Hrs Hudson says she cannot let because of damp; in this case, Mrs Hudson could presumably live at 221A or 221C....

13. *The Baker Street Boys* is a BBC series aired in 1983, with Jay Simpson as Wiggins, Roger Ostine as Sherlock Holmes and Huber Rees as Dr Watson.

Sherlock Holmes and The Baker Street Irregulars is a BBC drama, starring Jonathan Pryce as Sherlock Holmes and Bill Paterson as Dr Watson, released in 2007.

The Irregulars is a Netflix series, first aired in 2020, featuring Henry Lloyd-Hughes as Sherlock Holmes and Royce Pierreson as Dr Watson.

Christopher Morley famously wrote that 'The whole Sherlock Holmes saga is a triumphant illustration of art's supremacy over life.' (introduction to *The Penguin Complete Sherlock Holmes*).

14. Dorothy L. Sayers (1893–1957) was a founding member of both the Detection Club and The Sherlock Holmes Society (1934). She wrote extensively on Holmes, mainly for other fans, as well as producing her own novels, which were very successful but received some savage criticism in their day.
15. *The Inner Room* was first published in Conan Doyle's poetry collection *Songs of Action* (1898). It is an introspective exercise in which Conan Doyle sees himself comprising several different people, including a soldier and a priest, a 'rogue and an anchorite', and they all compete for domination of his soul.
16. The *Daily Telegraph* published his letter with the heading 'The Case of George Edalji – Special investigation by Sir A. Conan Doyle' on 6 January 1907.
17. For those interested in the case, Julian Barnes has written a best-selling novel, *Arthur and George* (Vintage 2006).
18. Conan Doyle wrote to the Spectator concerning several aspects of the case including a so-called 'confession' given by Slater and also saying that a man should be tried for the crime of which he was accused and not his moral character.
19. George Meredith (1828–1909) was an important but controversial Victorian poet and novelist. He was influential also with other writers as his poor sales meant he had to take work as a publisher's reader and read up to ten manuscripts a week. He is reputed to have been responsible for encouraging Thomas Hardy not to publish his first novel as it could be seen as 'socialistic' and ruin his career. Thomas Hardy then wrote *Far From the Madding Crowd* which was a best-seller and made his name.
20. Conan Doyle listed his personal favourites as follows:
    1. 'The Adventure of the Speckled Band' 1892
    2. 'The Red-headed League' 1891
    3. 'The Adventure of the Dancing Men' 1903
    4. 'The Final Problem' 1893
    5. 'A Scandal in Bohemia' 1891
    6. 'The Adventure of the Empty House' 1903
    7. 'The Five Orange Pips' 1891
    8. 'The Adventure of the Second Stain' 1904
    9. 'The Adventure of the Devil's Foot' 1910
    10. 'The Adventure of the Priory School' 1904
    11. 'The Musgrave Ritual' 1893
    12. 'The Adventure of the Reigate Squires' 1893
21. *Memories and Adventures* 1924
22. Arthur Balfour (1848–1930) was Prime Minister 1902–5. He also served as a Cabinet Minister for a total of twenty-seven years under Prime Ministers Asquith, Lloyd George and Baldwin. He may have said something often attributed to him: 'Nothing matters very much and few things matter at

all.' Conan Doyle wrote that of the 'occasional' great men that he had met, hardly anyone stood out more clearly. He was a very religious man and Conan Doyle was once a guest at Balfour's North Berwick estate when, on a Sunday night, maids, grooms, in fact all the staff of about twenty, and Balfour himself, conducted joint prayers. He was moved to see all, from the master of the house down to the most junior servant, praying as one. In life, nothing seemed more worthy of scorn to Balfour, Conan Doyle observed, than cowardice.

23. Herbert Henry Asquith, Prime Minister 1908–16, was the last leader of a majority Liberal government. Conan Doyle liked him greatly, especially his conversation, thinking him much maligned by people who said that he did not take the war seriously enough for the first two years during which he led the nation.

24. *David Copperfield* by Charles Dickens. The novel's full title is *The Personal History, Adventures, Experience and Observation of David Copperfield the Younger of Blunderstone Rookery (Which He Never Meant to Publish on Any Account)*, 1850 (previously serialised in monthly instalments from May 1849).

25. Details: *The World of Charles Dickens* by Stephen Browning (Halsgrove).

26. It was also at the Adelphi in December 1867 that Charles Dickens collaborated with his friend Wilkie Collins, to put on their play *No Thoroughfare*. It, too, was an enormous success running to over 150 performances and making a huge sum. Other Dickens productions included *The Christening* (1834), *The Peregrinations of Pickwick* or *Boz-i-a-na* (1837), *Nicholas Nickleby* (1838) and *The Old Curiosity Shop* (1840).

27. Dickens sets the beginning of his last great, unfinished, novel *The Mystery of Edwin Drood* in a drug den.

28. For many fans of the stories, this reaction of Watson is implausible. Yes, he is the most honourable and kindest of men, but Holmes had deceived him for three years in the most hurtful way imaginable. Watson's reaction in the BBC series *Sherlock* starring Benedict Cumberbatch and Martin Freeman, when he attempts to basically knock Holmes' block off received almost unstinting approval on social media.

29. Laurence Sterne's body was possibly the victim of grave-robbers and sold to anatomists at Cambridge University and was only reinterred after being recognised by someone who knew him in life. In the 1970s over 11,000 skulls were taken from this area when the land was redeveloped and one, with marks that would have been caused by anatomists and which was consistent with the size and shape of his bust, was found. This, and other remains, were reinterred at Coxwold churchyard in North Yorkshire.

30. Colonel Moran has spawned a huge amount of literature. There are many and an ever-growing number of Holmes' pastiches that introduce him. He has also been featured in novels, poems, TV series and films; notably George MacDonald Fraser introduces him in three of his *Flashman* books

and T.S. Eliot, in his poem *Gus: The Theatre Cat*, has Gus play a man-eating tiger who is chased down a drain by an Indian colonel – it was one of the legendary stories of late-Victorian society that Moran had fearlessly pursued a tiger in this manner.

31. The Marquess of Queensbury was acquitted; later Oscar Wilde was charged with gross indecency and sentenced to two years with hard labour.
32. Montague Street leads off Montague Place.
33. Watson, on the other hand, never sets foot in the British Museum as far as we know. On the principal occasion that he conducts research – into Chinese pottery in *The Adventure of the Illustrious Client* – he chooses to go to The London Library in St James's Square.
34. http://www.crossness.org.uk/
35. The complete list is: Bardle, Barton, Baynes, Bradstreet, Brown, Forbes, Forrester, Gregory, Gregson, Hill, Hopkins, Athelney Jones, Peter Jones, Lanner, Lestrade, MacDonald, MacKinnon, Martin, Merivale, Montgomery, Morton, Patterson and Youghal.
36. At the time of writing, eight of the twenty-four episodes filmed are available on YouTube, hugely enjoyable although the quality is not good. The series was filmed in Poland on a very tight budget, Reynolds using some scripts from his earlier and better known 1954 series starring Ronald Howard. At the end of filming the head of Polish television, who had authorised the production, was reportedly arrested and the film confiscated. The series never aired in the UK.
37. For analysis of the poem see the British Library www.bl.uk- romantic-and-victorians.
38. These include Chaucer, the first poet to be interred in the abbey. Some memorials have been delayed, for example, that of Lord Byron who had to wait almost 150 years before he was given one in 1969. Others include Edmund Spenser, George Handel, Charles Dickens, Ted Hughes, C.S. Lewis, Ben Johnson, Samuel Johnson, John Dryden, Robert Browning, Lord Tennyson, Rudyard Kipling, and Philip Larkin.
39. From *The Times* 14 June 1905 in an article entitled *Rifle Shooting as a National Pursuit*.
40. A Hull steam trawler, *Conan Doyle H240*, was named after Sir Arthur Conan Doyle and in 1917, under Skipper William Addy and Lieutenant McCabe, was involved for several hours in a fight with a German submarine and either sunk it or sent it under the waves in retreat. Skipper Addy was subsequently awarded the DSC. The ship sent Conan Doyle its ship's bell as a souvenir; he replied with his congratulations and a silver cigarette case inscribed with the skipper's name. Skipper Addy and the *Conan Doyle* also happened to hold the world record for the financial value of a trawler catch – £10,790.
41. reception@londonlibrary.co.uk. At time of writing, individual full membership is £510 a year. Special rates apply for young persons aged 16–26.

42. Graham Green wrote *The Return of A.J. Raffles* (1975) which was set in 1900 and included the characters of Lord Alfred Douglas and the Prince of Wales. In the play, Raffles and Bunny forge a plan to rob the Marquess of Queensbury, partly as revenge for his treatment of Oscar Wilde. Green said, 'I've brought out what I consider the latent homosexuality in the characters of Bunny and Raffles. I've done it only slightly—I mean it's not by any means a homosexual play.' It opened at the Aldwych Theatre on 4 December 1975, receiving rave reviews in some quarters for its sparkling dialogue. It has been produced many times since, including as a radio play for which it is particularly suited, by the BBC.
43. Julian Fellowes, or Baron Fellowes of West Stafford to give him his full title, is a best-selling author probably best known as creator, writer and producer of the worldwide success *Downton Abbey* (TV series 2010–15 and film 2019). He also appeared in two little-remembered, although highly entertaining, episodes of the Polish-British 1979 TV series *Sherlock Holmes and Dr Watson* with Geoffrey Whitehead as Holmes and Donald Pickering. as Watson, *A Motive for Murder* and *A Case of High Security*. Some of the series is available on YouTube.
44. Mark Haddon used the idea as the title of his award-winning novel *The Curious Incident of the Dog in the Night-Time* and the idea of a dog making a noise when sensing a stranger but keeping quiet when approached by someone it knows has been used in many subsequent crime stories.
45. Pierre Bayard: *Sherlock Holmes was Wrong: Re-opening the Case of the 'Hound of the Baskervilles'* (2007). Bayard, a French professor of literature, claims the hound to be totally innocent, the genuine human culprit slipping Holmes' grasp. This argument, of course, also implies that every reader of the tale was hoodwinked, too. Bayard argues that Conan Doyle, under pressure to bring back a character that he subconsciously hated, set Holmes up to fail. The book is ingenious, fun to read and the 'real' culprit will probably surprise you.
46. Details: *The World of Charles Dickens* by Stephen Browning (Halsgrove).
47. Angela Buckley has produced a fascinating book *The Real Sherlock Holmes – The Hidden story of Jerome Caminada* for Pen and Sword (2014).
48. After a chequered history during which it was very nearly turned into flats, 'Undershaw' was bought by The DFN Charitable Foundation for Stepping Stones School and was completely restored as far as possible to its original condition. The school was opened in 2016.
49. The other Holmes-recounted story is *The Blanched Soldier*. He did write, of course, and in the canon reports or monographs in his hand are mentioned on the following subjects: distinction between the ashes of various tobaccos; the tracing of footsteps; the influence of a trade upon the form of a hand; two studies on the human ear; the typewriter and its relation to crime; the Polyphonic Motets of Lassus; Practical Handbook of Bee Culture with some observations on the Segregation of the Queen; dating of documents; secret writings; and tattoo marks.

50. In *The Adventure of the Second Stain,* Watson begins the tale by saying that Holmes has since retired to keep bees on the Sussex Downs. We further learn, in the preface to *His Last Bow,* that this is at a small farm about five miles from Eastbourne.
51. For the list see www.arthur-conan-doyle.com.

Bibliography

Baring-Gould, William, *The Annotated Sherlock Holmes: The Four Novels and Fifty-six Short Stories Complete*, Clarkson Potter (1988)
Baring-Gould, William, S*herlock Holmes of Baker Street: A Life of the World's First Consulting Detective*, Bramhall House (1962)
Browning, Stephen, *The World of Charles Dickens*, Halsgrove (2012)
Browning, Stephen, *When Schooldays Were Fun*, Halsgrove (2010)
Buckley, Angela, *The Real Sherlock Holmes*, Pen and Sword Social (2014)
Conan Doyle Sir A., Stashower D., Lellenberg J., Foley C., *Arthur Conan Doyle: A Life in Letters*, Harper Perennial (2008)
Conan Doyle, Sir Arthur, *Memories and Adventures*, Project Gutenberg, Australia (2014)
Conan Doyle, Sir Arthur, *The Penguin Complete Sherlock Holmes*, Penguin Books (1981)
Duncan, Alistair, *An Entirely New Country*, MX Publishing (2011)
Hornung, E.W., *Raffles: The Amateur Cracksman*, Penguin Classics (2003)
Hornung, E.W., *The Complete Raffles Mysteries*, Createspace Independent Publishing Platform (2015)
Kirby, Dick, *Whitechapel's Sherlock Holmes*, Pen and Sword True Crime (2014)
Klinger, Leslie, *The New Annotated Sherlock Holmes: The Complete Short Stories: The Return of Sherlock Homes, His Last Bow and The Casebook of Sherlock Holmes*, W.W. Norton and Company (2007)
Lellenburg Jon, Stashower Daniel, Foley Charles, *Arthur Conan Doyle: A Life in Letters*, Harper Press (2007)
Lycett, Andrew, *Conan Doyle: The Man Who Created Sherlock Holmes*, W&N (2008)
Meyer Nicholas, *The Seven-Per-Cent Solution: Being a Reprint from the Reminiscences of John H. Watson*, E.P. Dutton (1974)
Morrisey S., Morrisey G., *The Complete Raffles, Annotated and Illustrated* (Kindle*)*, Amazon.com Services (2015)
Pascal, Janet B., *Arthur Conan Doyle: Beyond Baker Street*, Oxford University Press (2000)
Pearson, Hesketh, *Conan Doyle: His Life and Art*, Methuen (1943)
Read, Donald, *Edwardian England*, Harrap (1972)
Rowland, Peter, *Raffles and His Creator*, Nekta Publications (1999)

Stickler, Paul, *The Murder that Defeated Whitechapel's Sherlock Holmes*, Pen and Sword History (2018)

Wood, James P., *The Man Who Hated Sherlock Holmes. A Life of Sir Arthur Conan Doyle*, Pantheon Books (1965)

Interesting websites

www.Ihearofsherlockeverywhere.com Excellent for latest news of Sherlock and his world, especially as regards the USA.

arthur-conan-doyle.com For The Arthur Conan Doyle Encyclopaedia.

www.sherlockian.net Very good for all sorts of Sherlockian information.

bakerstreetirregulars.com Originally founded in 1934, The Baker Street Irregulars was the first Sherlockian literary society. It publishes the Baker Street Journal and is a wonderful source of information and events.

The Sherlock Holmes Society of London is a social and literary society and studies the life and work of Sherlock Holmes and John Watson. It is open to all. www.sherlock-holmes.org.uk

nationalarchives.org.uk for information on the history of the period.

Index

221B Baker Street, 17, 22–4, 25, 26, 39, 49, 50, 87, 90, 91, 117, 118, 129

A Case of Identity, 55, 57, 63, 74, 85, 91, 92, 94, 97, 110
A Scandal in Bohemia, 7, 33, 37, 45, 51, 94, 95, 110, 115, 126, 130
A Study in Scarlet, 3, 7, 15, 19, 22, 24, 26, 32, 45, 53, 63, 68, 94, 95, 97, 107, 110, 124, 125
Adelphi Theatre, 33, 40, 41, 131
Admiralty House, 77
Aldgate Station, 91
Alpha Inn, 59, 60
Arnold Bennett, 20, 21
Austen, Jane, 10, 61, 69

Baker Street, 15, 16, 20–1, 22, 24, 25, 36, 40, 42, 48, 53, 68, 71, 75
Baker Street Irregulars, 24, 118, 120, 122, 136
Balfour, Arthur, 36, 130–1
Bank of England, 85, 89
Bank tube station, 85, 88, 89, 90
Barbican, 86
Baring-Gould, William, 123, 135
Baskerville, Sir Henry, 34, 36, 48, 65, 77
Bazelgette, Joseph, 67
Beckenham, 98
Beeton's Christmas Annual, 3, 32
Bell's Life, 57
Berkshire, 94, 95, 98
Big Ben, 67, 70
Black Shuk, 10
Boer War, 9, 10, 76, 83

Bond Street, 49
Bow Street Police Station, 60
Bram Stoker, 1, 22
Brigadier Gerard, 7, 33, 41
British Empire, 17, 59, 67, 76
British Library, 14, 59, 81, 132
British Museum, 27, 55, 56, 58, 59–60, 132
Brixton, 98
Browning, Stephen, 131, 133, 135
Buckingham Palace, 46, 63, 64, 74, 77

Café Royal, 40, 53
Camberwell, 96, 97–8
Caminada, Detective Jerome, 106–7, 133
Cannon Street Station, 86, 90
Casement, Sir Roger, 12
Charing Cross, 34, 35, 37–9, 40, 53, 72, 79, 84, 102
Cholera, 24
Churchill, Winston, 22, 41, 81
Claridge's, 49, 50
Conan Doyle, Adrian, 11, 126
Conan Doyle, Kingsley, 3, 6, 12, 52
Conan Doyle, Knighthood, 9–10, 26, 74
Conan Doyle, Mary, 4
Conduit Street, 46, 51, 52
Cornhill Magazine, 4, 73
Cornwall, 94, 99
Cottingham Fairies, 12
Covent Garden, 24, 38, 55, 56, 60, 61–2
Cox and Co, 37, 72, 102

Craven Street, 36
Cricket, 1, 8–9, 26, 82, 96–7, 128
Criterion restaurant, 53
Cromer, 10, 108, 128
Croydon, 98
Cumberbatch, Benedict, 5, 68, 87, 113–14, 118, 122, 131
Curzon Square, 79, 81

David Copperfield, 38, 42, 61, 69, 128, 131
Devon, 94, 100–102
Dickens, Charles, 1, 7, 21, 22, 24, 32, 38, 40, 41, 42, 44, 57, 61–2, 69, 87, 104, 131, 132, 133, 135
Diogenes Club, 80, 81
Downey Jr, Robert, 5, 99, 114
Doyle, Kingsley, 3, 6, 12, 52
Draper Gardens, 90

Edalji George, 28–30, 130
Elementary, 5, 20, 69, 80, 103, 109, 118, 120, 123
Emma, 10, 69

Fenchurch Street, 86, 91, 92
Field, Charles Frederick, 61–2
Films, 5, 7, 19, 20, 41, 44, 66, 69, 84, 89, 93, 96, 99, 100, 101, 102, 112, 113, 114, 115, 116, 119, 120, 121, 131, 132, 133
Flat racing, 100
Fleet Street, 33, 34, 42–3, 62, 79
Forty Years of Scotland Yard, 93
Freeman, Martin, 5, 80, 114

Giant Rat of Sumatra, 88, 103, 109
Gillette, William, 7, 113, 115–16, 120, 128
Golden Cross Hotel, 37
Golden Jubilee Foot Bridges, 63, 64–5, 66
Goodge Street, 56, 57, 58
Great War, 3, 50, 52, 77

H.G. Wells, 11, 20–1, 22
Hampshire, 13, 94, 102
Hampstead, 48, 96
Hanover Square, 46, 51
Happisburgh, Norfolk, 107
Hard Times, 128
Hawkins, Louisa, 3
Haymarket, 45, 46, 54, 84
Herefordshire, 94, 103
His Last Bow, 11, 45, 50, 51, 111, 123, 134
Holdernesse, Duke of, 75, 77, 106
Holmes, Mycroft, 75, 77, 80, 91, 104, 117, 121, 123
Hornung E. W., 42, 78, 82–4, 96, 97
Houses of Parliament, 69–71

Johnson, Dr, 42–3, 82
Joseph Bell, 2, 18–19, 28

Kent, 61, 91, 94, 103, 104
Kyoto Teramachi Sanjo no Homuzu, 5

Law, Jude, 5, 98, 114
Leadenhall Street, 86, 91
Leckie, Jean, 7, 11
Lee (Kent), 91, 98
Lestrade, Inspector, 23, 51, 68, 79, 91, 97, 121, 132
Lewisham, 98
Lippincott's Monthly Magazine, 4, 72–3
Livanov, Vasily, 17, 50, 117–18
Lloyd George, 76, 130
Lombard Street, 90
London Library, 79, 81, 132
Lords Cricket Ground, 26, 96
Lower Norwood, 98
Lyceum Theatre, 7, 33, 62

Marble Arch, 46, 47, 48
Margate, 105
McKellen, Sir Ian, 19, 118, 121, 129
Memories and Adventures, 4, 5, 27, 40, 128

Midlands and North, 94, 105
Mincing Lane, 86, 92
Minories, 91
Miss Sherlock, 5, 20, 121
Montague Place, 27, 56, 58–9
Moran, Colonel Sebastian, 51–2, 131, 132
Moriarty, Professor, 8, 27, 49, 51, 87, 108, 119
Motoring, 76, 107–8
Mr Holmes (film 2015), 19, 118, 121, 129
Mrs Hudson, 8, 23, 24, 50, 52, 74, 87
Museum of London, 85, 88

National Gallery, 78, 79, 84
National Portrait Gallery, 78, 84
New Scotland Yard, 67, 68
Nihilists, 104
Nine Elms, 61, 98
Norbury, 98
Norfolk, 10, 27, 59, 80, 94
Northcliffe, Lord, 9
Northumberland Avenue, 33, 34–8, 40, 77, 79

Old Jewry, 88
Olympics, 9, 58
Oxford Street, 24, 45, 46, 47–50, 57, 62

Paddington, 72, 90, 95, 114,
Paget, Sidney, 5, 17, 18, 115
Pall Mall, 37, 77, 78, 79, 80
Park Lane, 46, 47–8, 49, 81
Parodies, 125
Pastiches, 37, 80, 88, 92, 97, 103, 109, 126, 131
Penge, 98
Pepys, Samuel, 61
Piccadilly Circus, 16, 45, 46, 53, 54, 84
Pycroft, Mr Hall, 90, 96, 105

Raffles, 42, 78, 82–4, 96, 97, 122, 133
Regent's Park, 15, 16, 26, 27
Regent Street, 45, 46, 48, 49, 50–3, 84
Reichenbach Falls, 6, 8, 34, 101, 129
Robinson, Bertram Fletcher, 101
Roosevelt, President Franklin D., 20
Roosevelt, President Theodore, 21, 43, 51
Rotherhithe, 98
Royal Opera House, 56, 60
Royalty, Sherlock Holmes and, 74–7
Russell Square, 56, 59

Sherlock (BBC series), 20, 68, 77, 80, 84, 87, 108, 113–14, 120, 122, 123, 125, 129, 131
Sherlock Holmes in the 22nd Century, 20, 107
Sherlock Holmes Pub, 36, 129
Sherlock: Untold Stories, 5, 20, 115
Sherlockolmitos, 88
Sholto, Thadeus, 62, 73
Siege of Sidney Street, 92–3
Silver Blaze, 49, 63, 73, 94, 95, 100, 110
Simpson's in the Strand, 41–2
Slater, Oscar, 30–1, 130
Smithfield Market, 85, 86–7
Soldiering, Conan Doyle and, 52, 76
Solomin, Vitaly, 17, 117
Somerset House, 42
Southsea, 21, 25, 52, 102
Speakers' Corner, 47
Spiritualism, 3, 7, 12, 13, 52, 97, 101
St Bartholomew's Hospital, 87–8
St James' Hall, 53
St John's Wood, 96
St Paul's Cathedral, 33, 34, 42, 43–4, 62, 79
Starrett, Vincent, 23
Stonyhurst, 1–2, 71

Strand Magazine, 6, 7, 10, 11, 13, 17, 23, 42, 83, 100, 102, 107, 108, 109, 115, 124
Streatham, 98
Surrey, 94, 98, 108–9
Sussex, 11, 13, 19, 25, 85, 88, 92, 94, 109, 111, 134
Sutherland, Miss Mary, 57, 91, 92, 97

Temple Bar, 3
The Adventure of Black Peter, 63, 75, 94, 109, 111
The Adventure of Charles Augustus Milverton, 45, 48, 63, 65, 75, 96, 111, 127
The Adventure of Shoscombe Old Place, 78, 81, 94, 95, 98, 111
The Adventure of the Abbey Grange, 63, 65, 78, 80, 94, 104, 105, 111
The Adventure of the Beryl Coronet, 15, 17, 90, 110
The Adventure of the Blanched Soldier, 85, 90, 111, 133
The Adventure of the Blue Carbuncle, 15, 19, 23–4, 45, 49, 55, 57, 59, 60, 63, 65, 97, 110
The Adventure of the Bruce-Partington Plans, 33, 39, 63, 74, 77, 85, 91, 111
The Adventure of the Cardboard Box, 55, 58, 63, 68, 94, 102, 110
The Adventure of the Copper Beeches, 55, 59, 94, 102, 106, 110
The Adventure of the Creeping Man, 94, 99, 111
The Adventure of the Dancing Men, 55, 59, 94, 107–8, 110, 130
The Adventure of the Devil's Foot, 15, 32, 94, 99, 111, 130
The Adventure of the Dying Detective, 8, 33, 41, 94, 98, 111
The Adventure of the Empty House, 45, 47, 51, 63, 75, 110, 123, 130
The Adventure of the Engineer's Thumb, 63, 68, 72, 94, 95, 110

The Adventure of the Golden Pince-Nez, 33, 38, 94, 104, 111
The Adventure of the Illustrious Client, 33, 35, 36, 40, 42, 45, 51, 53, 78, 81, 111, 132
The Adventure of the Lion's Mane, 94, 109, 111
The Adventure of the Mazarin Stone, 76, 85, 91, 111
The Adventure of the Missing Three-Quarter, 33, 39, 94, 99, 111
The Adventure of the Noble Bachelor, 33, 35, 45, 49, 51, 63, 74, 78, 79, 110
The Adventure of the Norwood Builder, 94, 98, 101, 110
The Adventure of the Priory School, 63, 75, 77, 94, 97, 105–6, 111, 124, 130
The Adventure of the Red Circle, 55, 58, 59, 60, 94, 96, 111
The Adventure of the Retired Colourman, 45, 54, 55, 94, 111
The Adventure of the Second Stain, 63, 71, 75, 94, 111, 130, 134
The Adventure of the Six Napoleons, 97, 111
The Adventure of the Solitary Cyclist, 8, 94, 108, 111
The Adventure of the Speckled Band, 8, 11, 33, 40, 42, 94, 108, 110, 130
The Adventure of the Sussex Vampire, 85, 88, 92, 94, 109, 111
The Adventure of the Three Gables, 45, 49, 78, 81, 111
The Adventure of the Three Garridebs, 32, 45, 47, 94, 105, 111
The Adventure of the Three Students, 94, 97, 99, 111
The Adventure of the Veiled Lodger, 94, 105, 111
The Adventure of Wisteria Lodge, 33, 38, 55, 60, 63, 74, 78, 81, 94, 108, 111
The Boscombe Valley Mystery, 94, 95, 96, 103, 110

Index

The Boy's Own Paper, 3
The Crooked Man, 63, 65, 110
The Disappearance of Lady Frances Carfax, 45, 49, 63, 68, 69, 94, 97, 111
The Final Problem, 7, 33, 39, 45, 49, 63, 73, 110, 116, 123, 130
The Five Orange Pips, 63, 65, 85, 91–2, 94, 98, 109, 110, 130
The 'Gloria Scott', 55, 59, 63, 77, 94, 107, 110
The Great Game, 26, 37, 49
The Great Stink, 24, 67, 70
The Greek Interpreter, 33, 35, 45, 53–4, 63, 77, 78, 80, 110
The Hope, 2
The Hound of the Baskervilles, 8, 10, 15, 22, 27, 33, 34, 36, 38, 39, 42, 45, 48, 49, 55, 60, 63, 65, 66, 77, 94, 100–101, 106, 108, 110, 112, 113, 114, 116, 117, 119, 120, 133
The Inner Room, 28
The Man with the Twisted Lip, 33, 44, 55, 60, 85, 90, 110
The Musgrave Ritual, 8, 55, 58, 63, 71, 74, 94, 110, 130
The Naval Treaty, 8, 63, 70, 75, 77, 108, 110
The Problem of Thor Bridge, 45, 49, 94, 102, 111
The Red-headed League, 32, 33, 43, 45, 53, 85, 86, 94, 105, 110, 130
The Reigate Puzzle, 94, 109, 110
The Resident Patient, 42, 45, 49, 110
The Sherlock Holmes Experience, 20
The Sherlock Holmes Museum, 15, 22, 25
The Sign of Four, 4, 8, 15, 24, 33, 43, 55, 62, 63, 68, 71, 72–3, 85, 92, 94, 98, 110, 116, 120, 123, 126
The Stark Munro Letters, 3
The Stock-broker's Clerk, 32, 94, 95, 96, 105, 110

The Strand, 22, 33, 34, 37–42, 62, 79, 87
The Valley of Fear, 11, 111, 120
The White Company, 4
The Whitehall Mystery, 67
The World of Charles Dickens, Stephen Browning, 131, 133
The Yellow Face, 15, 26, 110
Threadneedle Street, 17, 89, 90
Throgmorton Street, 90
Tibet, 123
Toby the dog, 98
Tottenham Court Road, 50, 55, 56–8, 96
Tower of London, 85, 86, 92
Trafalgar Square, 16, 34, 37, 38, 54, 63, 77, 78–80
Turkish Baths, 36, 49
Tyburn, 47

Undershaw, 22, 76, 108, 115, 133
University of Edinburgh, 2
Upper Wimpole Street, 15, 16, 27, 72

Victoria Street, 64, 72

W.G. Grace, 8–9, 97
Waller, Lewis, 41
Walsall, 28, 106
Waterloo station, 16, 34, 64, 65–6, 73
Wensley, Detective Inspector Frederick Porter, 92–3
Westminster Abbey, 63, 71
Westminster Bridge, 64, 68–70
Wilde, Oscar, 4, 21, 41, 53, 72–3, 82, 132, 133
Windlesham, 11, 13, 41, 71
Wordsworth, William, 69–70

Ye Olde Cheddar Cheese, 42–3, 82